Not easy being British: colour, culture and citizenship

Not easy being British: colour, culture and citizenship

Tariq Modood

tb

**Runnymede Trust and
Trentham Books**

First published in 1992 by Trentham Books Limited

Trentham Books Limited
Westview House
734 London Road
Oakhill
Stoke-on-Trent
England ST4 5NP

British Library Cataloguing in Publication Data
A catalogue record for this book is available from the British Library

ISBN: 0 948080 47 7

Cover photograph by Jon Walter

Designed and typeset by Trentham Print Design Ltd, Chester
and printed in Great Britain by BPCC Wheatons Ltd, Exeter.

For the children and especially for
Ghizala-Ruth and Yasmin-Cariad

'If you know nothing about a people,
you can believe anything'.
— Dervla Murphy

Acknowledgements

Most of these pieces were composed in my family time and I would like to thank my family, especially my wife, for sharing with me the conviction that this writing was worth doing.

I would also like to thank all of those friends and colleagues who have commented on parts of the contents and particularly Robin Richardson for his warm support and encouragement.

Thanks are also due to Nuffield College, Oxford and the Bestway Foundation for giving me the opportunity, in the form of a visiting Fellowship and a research grant respectively to finish the book and to pursue my writing further.

Contents

Preface

It's not easy being British: in articles, papers and reviews over the last few years Tariq Modood has documented some of the main problems. It is not easy to identify the values, processes and customs which are distinctively British; not easy, having identified them, to be in all respects proud, grateful and loyal; not easy to be recognised and accepted fully by other people who are British; not easy to establish and protect public policies and laws which recognise and rejoice that there are many different ways of being British, with sources of strength in different continents, religions, histories, languages.

One of Tariq Modood's pleas is that what he calls cultural-racism should be taken as seriously, and combated as rigorously, as colour-racism. It is a form of racism which has particularly significant and pernicious effects on the Muslim community.

'Islam, once a great civilisation worthy of being argued with,' wrote Peregrine Worsthorne in *The Sunday Telegraph* in February 1991, '... has degenerated into a primitive enemy fit only to be sensitively subjugated'. This was not only outrageous as a proposal for the present but also, in relation to the West's view of Islam in the past, amazingly inaccurate. For in point of fact, over the centuries, the West has been considerably more keen to subjugate Islam, and typically not at all sensitively, than to engage in argument and dialogue, or to engage in a joint enterprise of forming and reforming civilisation.

The West's view of Islam has of course to be understood as being more about the West's image of itself, and about the West's projects in history to 'subjugate' Islam, than about Islam. Over the centuries Westerners have seen themselves, in Edward Said's words, as 'rational, peaceful, liberal, capable of holding real values, without natural suspicion'. Arab-Orientals, however, says Said, are in Western eyes 'none of these things'. The West's grand narrative is mainly moral, cultural and theological in its expressions, but has never, as Said documented at length in his book *Orientalism,* been wholly separate from patterns and structures of military conflict. In the late twentieth century it is of course not wholly separate from geopolitical factors to do with energy supplies, or from threats to the security of Israel.

Nor is anti-Islamic feeling separate from the socio-economic location of Muslim communities in the societies of Western Europe. In Britain, for example, Muslims suffer more than do other ethnic minority communities from poor housing, poverty, unemployment and low educational achievement, and from immigration policies which keep families apart. 'Orientalism', in Said's term, is in its current form a way of legitimising Muslim poverty and disadvantage; of preventing the reunification of Muslim families; and of ensuring that Muslims are unable to take a full part in the social, economic, cultural and political life of mainstream society.

The intellectual task of challenging, correcting and re-writing the grand narrative involves major historical studies such as Edward Said's *Orientalism*. Also, and extremely importantly, it involves vigilantly watching current events as they unfold in specific historical and social circumstances, and vigilant attention to the texts — books, articles, lectures, speeches, journalism — which they generate, and through which they are interpreted. Such vigilance has been the hallmark of Tariq Modood's book reviews and academic articles. In one piece of occasional writing after another he has noted watchfully what is happening in British culture and society, and has issued warnings, offered reflections, made suggestions.

In gathering together some of his recent writings, the Runnymede Trust and Trentham Books hope to extend the sphere in which Tariq Modood's ideas are known and attended to. He challenges much conventional thinking on 'race' equality issues, and highlights a number of new priorities and needs for the years ahead. Recurring emphases in these pages include the following:

— 'cultural racism' is separate from as well as interwoven with 'colour racism', and often needs to be addressed as a distinct issue;

— 'racial dualism', which involves categorising everyone as either 'black' or 'white', provides therefore an inadequate theoretical framework, and an inadequate agenda for practical action;

— religious faith is an integral part of the identity of many oppressed people, and is a source of strength for them: it cannot be dismissed as mere delusion or mere so-called fundamentalism;

— we need in Britain to develop the concept of hyphenated identity (Black-British, Muslim-British, Indian-British, etc);

— we need to take account of 'the ethnicity paradox': the fact that the long road away from racism and towards racial equality and justice has often to go through spaces where people can know and take pride in their own distinctive history, narratives, language, tradition;

— we need also, however, to explore and develop the concept of commonality — the interests, values, symbols, rituals, ceremonies, stories and sentiments which large numbers of British people of different ethnicities can share and jointly affirm.

It's not easy being British in the 1990s. In an article in the *Spectator* in October 1991 Charles Moore argued for an explicitly racist immigration policy.

Britain should not, he said, permit people with dark skins to settle here. He made it clear, at the same time, that he objected not only to dark skins but also to non-Christian religions, specifically to Islam, and to languages other than English. 'You can be British without speaking English or being Christian or being white,' he conceded, but added: 'Nevertheless Britain is basically English-speaking, Christian and white, and if one starts to think it might become urdu-speaking and Muslim and brown, one gets frightened and angry'. He went on to argue that Britain should open its doors to Poles and Hungarians and Russians, 'in the hope that one day we could return to the situation before 1914 in which you could travel from Paris to St Petersburg without a passport. Muslims and blacks, on the other hand, should be kept out as strictly as at present'. This pairing of all blacks with all Muslims was a pairing of biological and cultural racism, reminiscent in this respect of anti-semitism. Moore's article closed with a further explicit reference to his view that Islam is biologically foreign to the West, with a wholly different bloodstream:

> 'Because of our obstinate refusal to have babies, Western European civilisation will start to die at the point when it could have revived with new blood. Then the hooded hordes will win, and the Koran will be taught, as Gibbon famously imagined, in the schools of Oxford.'

If such nonsense is to be adequately combated, it will be vital that entirely different accounts of history and reality are provided and attended to. Tariq Modood's account, unfolded through his occasional writings in response to specific events and publications, is one which everyone interested in British society and culture needs to attend to. His account can help all of us, whatever our own personal history, connections and perspectives (whatever, that is to say, our own hyphenated identities) to work with the difficulties of being British, and of working for a time when being British is less stressful, and less problematic, than at present.

Robin Richardson
Director, The Runnymede Trust

Voices in a moral dialogue

1

Biography and Identity: an essay in personal and social history

My father has long been of the view that the idea of an English gentleman comes very close to what the Qur'an requires from the individual. One of his favourite sayings is 'God made man but a tailor makes a gentleman'. This led to on-going rows between us over my style of dress, especially in my teens and when I was a student. Some years later — and this is the point of the example — when I was still dressing as a layabout as he saw it, he said to me: 'You haven't turned out too badly'. He came to see that while I did not share his sartorial standards, we shared many common values and that I held some of the standards of conduct that he had sought to inculcate. That under my hippie exterior there was courtesy, gentleness in speech and sobriety; there was commitment to honour one's word and fulfil one's obligations, not to defame others or act out of malice or ulterior motive; and, as a further example, there was a valuing of education for its contribution to one's soul and for the opportunities it gives to serve others less talented or socially fortunate. Common values can therefore belie differences in outward appearance. The example may also illustrate the many cases of inter-generational culture-clash in immigrant families capable of resolution. My example is idiosyncratic but it should not be dismissed.

Recently, I was involved in a BBC Radio 4 programme and the producer challenged me to take my ideas back to my former school in the London Borough of Brent. It was a secondary modern when I went there and in many ways a typical inner city school. It has always been working class, but when I first went it was very much a white school. Its composition dramatically changed during my years there and now only 10% of the pupils are white and over 50% are from an African-Caribbean background. Radio 4 arranged for an 'A' level English literature class to discuss a passage which I thought

3

embodied some English values, but which it was possible for anyone to make their own. I chose the ideal of a 'parfit gentil knyght', knowing that it would seem remote, that students would find fault with it, and that it would immediately raise Muslim hackles — and yet I believe it was capable of appreciation on reconsideration. The passage was from the General Prologue of Chaucer's *The Canterbury Tales* and can be summed up in the following extract:

> A Knyght ther was, and that a worthy man
> That fro the tyme that he first bigan
> To riden out, he loved chivalrie,
> Trouthe and honour, freedom and curteisie.
> Ful worthy was he in his lordes werre,
> And therto hadde he riden, no man ferre,
> As wel in cristendom as in hethenesse,
> And evere honoured for his worthynesse.

They thought it was sexist, Euro-centric, Christian-centric, highly classist and harking back to an England that had never existed. I then asked them to tell me their values which they started to list: truth-telling, respect for elders, courtesy, consideration for others, self-control, being true to oneself and (most interestingly) they blamed the television for too much sex, violence and swearing. For a moment I closed my eyes and could hear my father talking. My point is that multi-culturalism must rest on an affirmation of shared moral certainties: it cannot just be about differences. We have a lot in common and must work to bring this out. Some of the moral certainties would be to do with the family, community, religious or quasi-religious ethics. The Swann Report, the major British document on multi-culturalism, emphasised the importance of developing a common framework of values; while it took too antipathetic a view on the contribution of religious schools to this end, and gave no thought to how we were to move from values we *do* share to the values it believed we *should* share if a rational pluralist society is to be established, the emphasis on common values is too much neglected by the Report's admirers and detractors, and needs far more attention than it has received hitherto.

If it was possible for my father to think of me, long-haired, tie-less and in my tight fading jeans as a gentleman, then although outward appearances may change, there can be a continuity of values. Even at the time when Chaucer wrote *The Canterbury Tales* people would have said that his concept of gentilesse was very aristocratic. He was, however, attempting to lift it out of its social setting and to show that it had nothing intrinsically to do with aristocracy. Likewise, with our concepts of Britishness, Hinduness, Muslim-ness, Africanness, or whatever else that people think is under threat as an identity in contemporary Britain. We have to find a new way of affirming what is worthwhile and of value to us, but which cannot survive in outdated forms without seeming to exclude or create separatism.

For members of minorities, individual self-esteem critically hangs upon group dignity and group status. Some of the dimensions of the Salman Rushdie Affair reflect this kind of besieged insecurity on the part of Muslims who feel they are not valued or respected. Expecting minorities to fit into categories, even well-meaning ones, devised by others can be a further source of resentment. People thought to be 'black' may turn round and demand to be recognised as Muslims — with all that implies for educational and welfare policies. In many ways the respect that individuals seek is tied up with the respect their group receives, so it is very difficult for individuals to have some sense of their own worth when the group they belong to is being systematically disparaged and devalued. Asking the minorities to 'assimilate' in the context of widespread racial discrimination is asking for conflict and destabilisation and the fragmentation of communities that are currently the sources of stability, group pride and self-esteem. Even ignoring the question of rights, it is therefore bad social policy to insist upon assimilation. What we really need are new concepts of Britishness.

We could here learn something from the Americans who have come to have a notion of *hyphenated nationality*. They take pride not just in their Americanness but in asserting that they are Irish-American, Black-American, African-American, Greek-American and so on. And when a presidential candidate can make the assertion of being a Greek-American an explicit part of his campaign, it is clear that a hyphenated nationality does not imply that one is only half-American or any detraction from patriotism. Rather, it is seen as the claiming of an ethnic identity within the framework of a common nationality that is open to all forms of ethnic difference that do not challenge the over-arching bonds of nation and citizenship. 'British' by contrast is virtually a quasi-ethnic term, and being closely identified with 'whiteness', it excludes other ethnic terms, so it is not surprising that descriptions such as British Black or British Pakistani are at present not much more than courtesy titles and carry limited conviction. What we need, therefore, contrary to the reinforcement of ethnocentricity in the national curriculum, are ways to move towards a concept of Britishness that is not frozen in history and identified with only one or a narrow set of ethnicities, such as English, Welsh, Scottish and Irish, but can highlight the grounds of our commonality, past and present, as well as our contribution through our differences.

An explicit form of our commonality is our common citizenship, that we are members of the same national state or commonalty. I think we make too little of this and need to give more valued expression to it than we do. We need a demonstrative expression of commonalty and national loyalty that can serve as a symbol of belonging. The Americans have this in the American Constitution and in the acceptance of this constitution as the condition of citizenship. They also insist upon single nationality. Quite contrary to what I was saying about being Greek-American, which is a form of being American, you cannot be Greek and American in the sense of holding a Greek passport and an American passport. For us to have exactly what the Americans have

5

got would be too simplistic because there is genuine value in having dual-nationality, for it allows individuals and families to straddle countries and link economies. What is important is that the Americans have had — and recognise — the importance of having the means whereby people can say: 'I too am American because I go along with that, so don't tell me about loyalty tests. I am American just like you because there is something we can point to as the basis of our commonality and nationality.'

In this sense, Americans are more open to diversity than the British and yet are very definite about there being unity, everyone being able to assert that their being American means more than happening to live inside the borders of the USA. Lawrence Fuchs in a masterful survey of ethnicity in America celebrates the impulse to diversity in American society, arguing that contemporary America is probably one of history's best examples of a society making diversity work (Fuchs, 1990). Yet an important strand of his argument is that the acceptance of the American constitution and the political culture that goes with it has been such a powerful vehicle for demonstrating allegiance to America by new groups that it has neutralised the forces of majoritarian cultural intolerance. In short, a demonstrative loyalty to the republic and its constitutional principles created the space for religious and cultural diversity, and for the visible formation of tight ethnic residential communities and ethnic origin-based interest groups at all levels of American society.

Britain is sufficiently different from USA in its political culture, immigration, demography and much else for us not to attempt US solutions here in any crude sense. There may also be some romanticism in Fuchs' view. Yet there is some sense in the idea that by insisting on adherence to the national ideology that informs the political institutions one makes the commonalty a secure basis for the expression of commonality, and thereby takes the pressure off new minorities to exhibit loyalty through socio-cultural conformity in everyday life. For ethnic minorities in Britain there is bound to be some attraction in the idea that one Loyalty Test should replace numerous less explicit loyalty tests. For the pressures to conform in Britain are greater than they are in America, even though, admonitions from Home Office ministers notwithstanding, there is little official pressure that people must become 'British'. The pressures are social and cultural rather than legal, political or institutional. On the one hand, we are more culturally intolerant towards minority differences. On the other hand, we are wholly unspecific about forms of loyalty, even at a symbolic level.

The American example (or, as it may be, an idealised version of it), however, has its limitations. It is not at all easy to place the burden of community upon allegiance to the commonalty. The Americans have achieved it by a powerful national ideology, virtually a civil religion, vindicated by economic abundance and super-power glory. We cannot reproduce those conditions here. Nor is Britain a wholly secular state. It is better that our state schools contribute to nation-building by beginning the day with collective religious worship that all may participate in (the direction schools were headed in before the ethnocentric Education Reform Act) rather than, as in America, by saluting the flag.

A citizenship of legal rights must be at the heart of any democratic conception, but it cannot exist without other forms of commonality. Moreover, as different minorities overlap with each other and the broader society in different ways, each of these overlaps needs to be secured and built upon. We must find commonality where we can and extend it, so that shared values at one level (say, personal morality) can be of some balance against divisions elsewhere, for example, the inevitable political conflicts that go with the demand for equal rights.

The current fashion of criticising Muslims and others for organising along religious lines to press for civil rights is a secular prejudice. A liberal society is no more pro or anti political mobilisation on the basis of religious affiliation than it is on the basis of class or race or gender. What destroys liberal citizenship is if any one of these collective modes always trumps the others; if people come to inhabit any one of these modes to the exclusion of the others such that deep social divisions are formed and the free criss-crossing association of individuals necessary for a common citizenship is difficult. In the last 150 years or so, class has been the greatest challenge to liberals; the new political significance of other collectivities provides a welcome pluralism. Liberals ought not to despise the faiths of minority communities and their contribution to a healthy pluralism. The radical secularism of some reformers threatens to ghettoise all religions by obliging each religious community to set up a system of educational provision outside the state. This American approach will create greater communalism than most British people want; it would be better to give the minority religions a public dignity and role consonant with their importance to social cohesion. Racial minorities, which in many cases means religious minorities, ought to be pulled in to the state, not kept out.

We need an educational philosophy which recognises that individuals and communities have a right to be culturally different from their neighbours and to be understood in their own terms and not in terms of racist and anti-racist stereotypes. This inevitably means creating a positive awareness of multi-culturalism in all pupils, majorities and minorities. It implies a recognition of the inadequacy of an anti-racism in education which narrowly focuses on colour and class and fails to engage with cultural-racism. The right to cultural difference also means creating the educational space for minorities to do their own thing. This extends to policy decisions such as the inclusion within the state sector of Muslim and other minority faith denominational schools where they satisfy the requirements of the national curriculum and of DES standards of efficiency. Those worried by the low educational standards of some private Muslim schools should bear in mind that there is nothing inevitable about low standards. There are Muslim schools in America which have quickly established themselves as superior to the education provided by the public school system. In any case, if private Muslim or other religious schools are

7

proving to be educationally inadequate that surely is an argument for allowing them into the more regulated sector. There are unlikely to be many such schools, but they will meet the needs of the particularly orthodox, remove a community grievance of unequal treatment and, like all educational experiments, provide a resource for the rest of the system to learn from and selectively use.

The development carries a risk of communalism, but this can be countered by the development of some genuine multi-faith schools; if such schools are to be more than just nominal Christian or secular schools with multi-faith rolls they will need to be part of a larger multi-faith movement. Educational rights for cultural minorities also extend to the provision of community languages within the timetable. Giving those children who want it the option of, for example, Urdu instead of French, may be to decrease their subsequent career opportunities in the post-1992 world but this is a choice that pupils and their parents should be able to make. Yet the aim of multi-culturalism as an educational and social philosophy should not be to reinforce separate identities but to give enough confidence to all not to be ashamed of one's ethnic background, to be able to celebrate it while respecting that of others, and above all to give to each person enough confidence in their group identity so as to be able to cross boundaries and to share others' cultures. If this aim seems contradictory in itself or with the examples I have given, it is an illustration of what has been called 'the ethnicity paradox': one needs a certain amount of conservative autonomy in order to create the psychologically and sociologically secure identities which will be open to change and synthesis, and will be able to contribute something of their own to the wider society and not be swamped by it. The pluralism that should be our goal must be open to change and should allow individuals some degree of choice. For not only are most minority individuals bi-cultural or even multi-cultural, but most people do not want to be tied to the culture of their origins or families in accordance with the preconception of others, especially outsiders to that community. Many Asian and black people are at home in and identify themselves with majority British cultural styles and this too is part of a natural diversity. It can be no part of pluralism that individuals are pressed into narrow pigeon-holes which others believe they should be in because of their ethnic origins or appearance.

The right to be culturally different, to be a minority, has I have argued to be balanced against the fact of being a society. One of the most basic functions of education is induction into the common society. This must go well beyond the imparting of a standard of English and numeracy, and all the other skills necessary for adult employment and basic social survival. It is sometimes suggested that what is needed is preparation for democratic citizenship. While there is something right in this, it cannot be interpreted too abstractly for after all one is talking about *this* democracy and *this* citizenship. Just as American citizenship rests on a particular constitution with its own particular founding myths and a historically developed political culture, so similarly our commonality, our common future, has to be shaped by our understanding of and commitment to our commonalty. Differences can only flourish where one can take a certain amount of commonality for granted: it must be the task of our schools to make both these things possible. To do so is to extend and enrich our understanding of our Britishness, a sense of belonging capable of embracing a number of hyphenated nationalities; we will need the assistance of the moral and religious traditions that at least partly constitute what we mean by ethnicity. These traditions are not about to fade away and must be co-opted into the classroom as into our social order. They are, underneath their alien and divisive appearance, part of our commonality which is in the making and cannot be ghettoised into some private realm. Together with the challenge of eliminating racism, they offer the basis of a morally strengthened social order. Indeed, these are at bottom not two separate tasks: multi-cultural education is a significant way to challenge racism, especially cultural-racism, by tackling its intellectual and moral roots. Educationalists have a leading role in moving the perception of ethnic minorities in terms of colour and class to voices in a moral dialogue. They will need to proceed by doing some listening.

This paper was given to a conference on Education for Citizenship held at the Institute of Education, University of London, in association with the Runnymede Trust, 30 November 1991. For a fuller argument, see Modood 1992a.

2

Islam and Western Humanism: the need for mutual learning

Review of **A Faith for All Seasons: Islam and Western Modernity**, Shabbir Akhtar, Bellew Publishing.

Most young educated Muslims in Britain, in so far as they are concerned to be Muslims, use Islam as a basis of individual and community self-defence; few, though post-Rushdie affair increasingly, use it as a basis of wounded assertiveness, for counter-attack against the ubiquitous hegemony of western culture. Shabbir Akhtar goes well beyond both of these types of question-begging, holier-than-thou apologetics, and the tone and content of this book will surprise both his critics and admirers. His passionate opposition to *The Satanic Verses* has earned him the reputation of a fanatic and casuistical defender of the indefensible, yet this book, evidently some time in the maturing, is a sober and reasoned plea for Muslims to face up to and learn from modern western thought. The spirit of grievance and enmity has almost entirely given way to one of self-critical inquiry, with harsh words being almost wholly reserved for conservative Muslims.

Modern Islam has produced a few, too few, practical reformers, such as Syed Ahmed Khan, Mohammed Abduh and Fazlur Rahman, keen to update Islamic customs, ethics, education and laws, and in Iqbal alone a speculative metaphysician at home with the western philosophy of his day. Akhtar is one of the first to attempt to map the ground that Muslims must cover if they are to re-think their faith and situate themselves in post-Enlightenment culture. His patient and scrupulous analysis serves to construct a conceptual framework in which there can be an intelligent dialogue between Islam and western modernity.

Akhtar is willing to engage with and learn from liberal Protestant theology and biblical scholarship, described as 'the finest essay in intellectual probity in the history of religious ideas', and appreciates the efforts of Orientalists who have attempted to do the same with the Qur'an, though he argues that

11

their lack of sympathy for the texts they study makes their value limited. He recognises the important intellectual, cultural and even spiritual contribution made by atheism, seems to have a special admiration for Nietzsche, and is thoroughly familiar with contemporary Anglo-American analytical philosophy of religion — indeed, Grey Seal has just published *The Light in the Enlightenment*, Akhtar's 'forceful defence of Christianity'. It is interesting to note that while Akhtar's call to Muslims to come to terms with the secular and sceptical spirit of our times is in the Islamic context a courageously liberal stand, among Christian philosophers he sides with the conservatives (perhaps a no less courageous position).

A key example of Akhtar's re-interpretation of Islam is his analysis of rejection of faith. The Qur'an speaks of rejection as a form of hypocrisy, at best a self-deception, for it does not entertain the idea that rejection can be sincere, reasoned or out of an anguished reflection on the extent of purposeless suffering in the world. Akhtar, on the contrary, argues that these are all genuine possibilities, which often reflect a more serious moral engagement than that exhibited by the believer for whom the question of doubt has not arisen; hence 'a modern Muslim cannot take all his cues from the Koranic attitude to rejection'. Modern humanist thinkers can only be construed as *kaffir* where there is, in one of the most memorable phrases of the book, a 'bloody-minded will to obscurantism'. This argument about the limited assistance of the Qur'an in interpreting modern categories of thought is by no means confined to the issue of rejection. The general message is that 'so much that we see around us today is beyond the good and evil of our forefathers'.

Yet while the thrust of the book is to emphasise a break with the past, especially the modern Muslim past, there is also an appeal to a lost purity. On the one hand, Islam is described as a raw material which must be suitably historicised, for 'we must adapt it, change it, perhaps even eventually transform it, all within the flux of history'. On the other hand, Akhtar claims that his 'attempt at a reverent scepticism in these pages is in the service of rediscovering the old Islam'. There is of course nothing intrinsically wrong in having it both ways. It may indeed be true that each of these attitudes is appropriate for different parts of Islam. The problem then is to establish the criteria for deciding when to be modern and when to be fundamentalist. In the long uncompleted retreat of European cultural imperialism it is not surprising that oppressed peoples conscious of proud pre-colonial histories should imagine a return to a golden age, yet the value of these sources of pride can only be that they lead to a successful engagement with new concepts, priorities and circumstances. I am less than optimistic that the current 'return to fundamentals' movement among Muslims is having this effect.

Unlike most self-professed fundamentalists, Akhtar has an acute understanding of a religion other than his own. His discussions of the tragic vision of man in Christianity and of why it worships suffering love as the highest quality of God are cases in point. Yet he sees Christianity too much in terms of an Augustinian pessimism. For while Christians have not been inclined to give human reason the importance ascribed to it in the Qur'an, the shift in Christianity from social pessimism to social idealism predates the Enlightenment. It is most evident for example in the 17th century radical Puritans (such as the Levellers) to whom contemporary Islamic fundamentalists bear considerable likeness (though without the emphasis on individual conscience and salvation). It is the individualism of Christianity and the cultures that it has given rise to that is one of its most distinctive features. For the idea of the individual soul as an end-in-itself is no less central to Christian metaphysics than the idea of divinity as self-sacrificial love and finds its best modern philosophical expression in Kant. Islam, on the other hand, centres on Creation, Reason and Law, and offers the kind of communitarian theosophy in which Hegel could have felt at home.

One unsatisfactory feature of Akhtar's approach is the short shrift he gives to the idea of Christian-Muslim dialogue, describing it as no more than a reciprocal exercise in 'Know they enemy'. It is almost as if he thinks that Islam can learn from liberal humanism without compromising itself but a dialogue with other faiths, especially Christianity, is necessarily a competitive relationship best carried out at arm's length. The scars from missionary arrogance and disdainful orientalism are most evident at this point. Yet the one group to have made a real attempt to understand the complex feelings of British Muslims over the Rushdie affair, and to call for protection of minority sensibilities, is the Christian-led inter-faith movement. It is a pity that a book which can profoundly widen Muslim sensibilities and intellectual horizons should end on an ungenerous note.

Source: *The Times Higher Education Supplement*, 22 March 1991

3

Tales from Two Cities: messages for the 1990s

Review of **Tales from Two Cities**, Dervla Murphy, John Murray.

Intelligence. A practical judgement which is able to hold its own against dogma and political myth-making. A perseverance happily combined with a breadth of character which together, despite all conceivable obstacles, is able to engage with the humanity of others. These are some of the outstanding qualities found in virtually every page of Dervla Murphy's *Tales from Two Cities*. Oh, and honesty and the courage it takes to broadcast unpopular truths.

Dervla Murphy is a distinguished travel writer of journeys, usually requiring physical courage, in South Asia, Africa and South America. She has also written on the communal conflicts of Northern Ireland — she herself is Southern Irish. Her latest book is based upon living most of 1985 amongst the Mirpuris in Manningham, Bradford and in multi-racial Handsworth, Birmingham, especially with blacks including the Rastas at the Villa Cross pub. Just as the average Briton knows little more about Northern Ireland than that it is a problem, so that same person knows little more about the non-whites in Britain other than that 'they' are a problem. Their only newsworthy feature is their latest version of giving offence.

Ms Murphy's insistence that racism — of which she comes across plenty — cannot be opposed by those who do not make the effort to understand it, leads her to uncover the depths of mutual ignorance that exist between the different communities that now live side by side, and which leads to communities living in mental — and sometimes physical — ghettoes reminiscent of Belfast. This aspect of her philosophy is eloquently encapsulated in one sentence: 'If you know nothing about a people, you can believe anything'. Having spent a year in Belfast I can certainly testify to how some Protestant and Catholic school-leavers — who may never have met anyone of the opposed denomination — are capable of believing extraordinarily hateful, and sometimes just plain silly, things about each other.

In seeking to understand the variety of non-white experience in her two chosen cities, she creates a rapport with a host of individuals. The book is a rich tapestry of real life stories with real characters and complications and not just political stereotypes — though no effort is made to hide our faults (Asian male readers who think sex equality is too 'advanced' an idea had better skip pp. 21-28).

Her accounts of the Honeyford affair and the Handsworth riots, which took place during her sojourn, are fascinating though often depressing. Her ability to see different sides of highly emotive issues furthers our understanding at just those moments when one is likely to see those issues merely in terms of racism or law and order. Sometimes, however, one cannot help but cheer as the truth stands up out of the page — with the young Sikh, for example, who angrily blurts out 'I am not black' even though he knows Asians are not meant to say such things.

Sympathetic commentators on race normally see non-white people in white society as objects of pity or as raw materials to be worked up for political purposes. Dervla Murphy actually records some of our social virtues. Thus we see Asian self-reliance, emotional solidarity, school and career ambitions in a context of industrially run-down inner cities, side by side with whites dependent upon over-stretched welfare services, lacking all hope and giving up on the up-bringing of their children. She warns, however, that these qualities — family and community strength, hard work, discipline, resourcefulness — risk decay in such an environment or, if denied a legitimate public recognition, could be put to use in urban violence.

There are parallels here with West Indians. The pages on Handsworth contains a very good presentation of the current attitudes and debates of the black community, including that section that rarely achieves mass media publicity, the deeply church-going. This half of the book also holds up a microphone to those Asians caught between theft, intimidation and violence from some blacks and a total unresponsiveness from the white police. One of the most moving passages in the book is of Asian men weeping as their shops are looted and years of family hard work and sacrifice are put to the flame.

In contrast to Handsworth, Ms Murphy is struck by the depth and pervasiveness of racial prejudice amongst white Bradfordians. She apportions some of the blame to the political naivety and hostility-provoking activities of Bradford's anti-racists. Her blow-by-blow account of the Honeyford affair reveals how good causes can be badly managed, how victories can be bought at too high a price and how we can become political footballs kicked betwixt Left and Right. Both these political groups have chosen to make us a battleground. Indeed, Asian and black people are at present to the hard Left and the New Right what West Germany is to NATO and the Warsaw Pact respectively. Not surprising that many of us are chilled by our anti-racist Cold War style warriors who look not for a thaw but a hot war; and, like the West

Germans, 'victory' frightens us more than the status quo. Indeed, better Red than dead.

The book itself is a brilliant demonstration of the antidote to prejudice, the effort of understanding. It has got to be said, however, that the problems of racial inequality go beyond this antidote. While Dervla Murphy does not attempt to offer any political solutions, it seems to me that her book does provide important materials for political reflection. The problem seems to be that without political intervention, racial inequality and ghettoisation will become permanent features of British society. Yet previous generations of ethnically different immigrants came to establish themselves despite being initially met by prejudice, discrimination, low status and exclusion. And they did it without any special political measures. Hence current British society thinks the latest immigrants should 'prove' themselves and adapt in the same way.

Under these circumstances the sensible option for groups like ourselves is to campaign for political action on racial inequality in a manner which will be persuasive to a sceptical electorate (discounting the downright hostile) and premised on time-frames based upon studies of real cases (from British or American history) of how long it takes 'out-groups' to become 'in-groups'. For some inner-city groups in areas where jobs will not return fast enough, such patience and long-term vision may no longer be possible and 'what the hell' conflict may become routine. Yet the virtues that Asian communities have already demonstrated suggest that at least some groups are capable of achieving disciplined, steady progress. Though it is worth underlining that Ms Murphy's sees this underlying framework of discipline, at least in the case of Muslims, as derived from their religion; so that if, as Mohammed Ajeeb predicts, the new generation is 'unable to withstand Western values and culture', then she forecasts that the transitional hiatus between rejection of traditions of social discipline and the acquisition of self-discipline is a critical period of risk, when the attitude of white society will determine the destinies of all of us.

Source: *Asian Herald*, 19 April 1988

4

Equality Professionals and Ethnic Identity: a memorandum to colleagues

Can whole groups of people be Chinese and not know it? Or Greek Cypriot? Or black? Many people will find these questions absurd. Such people do not deserve to be working in equal opportunities.

For to find these questions absurd is to be so comfortably cocooned in equal opportunities rhetoric as to be ignorant of the fact that the majority of non-white people in Britain today find themselves in this predicament. They don't know they are black but find themselves referred to as such by race equality professionals and politicians.

Why do these professionals insist that non-white means black? The standard argument is that it facilitates a necessary coalition amongst ethnic minority groups in order to oppose racism. However, it does so at the price of asking the numerically larger party to this coalition, the Asians, to adopt an identity false to their own being. Only a fool would want to build a coalition on these terms if they were serious about it lasting. For it is obvious that Asians will only accept such a deal to the extent that they feel they have no option. Such a unity will be only skin-deep and will be — is being — betrayed at the first opportunity. It would surely be more advantageous in the long run to emulate Jesse Jackson's 'Rainbow Coalition' which invites all non-white US ethnic minorities to forge a common political purpose without any of the groups being obliged to subordinate their ethnicity to a political identity.

That this is not the dominant view amongst British race egalitarians can't be because they oppose ethnicity. For example, they applaud the desire amongst some African-Caribbeans to create a black ethnic identity rooted in their African origins. An example is the musical *Black Heroes in the Hall of Fame*, acclaimed for its contribution to black pride, and yet there are no

Asians in this hall of fame — not because of any hostility but simple because they not 'true' blacks.

It is time for all honest race egalitarians critically to examine why it has become an article of faith that all non-whites must be 'black'. For what is the common positive identity behind the idea of 'black'? Of course Asians and blacks both suffer the same racial discrimination by white society, but that is a negative condition. It describes how others mistreat us, not what we understand and value ourselves to be. It is often said 'racists have no trouble in saying who is black, so why should we?' as if racists are to have the last word on the matter.

Most people wish to put on show their best features, those qualities in which their individual and collective pride resides and by which they want the rest of the world to know them. They wish to be known for what they are, not for what others find problematic about them.

The inherent difficulties in the idea of 'black' are evidenced by the fact that few Asian, black nor white people use this term consistently. Black people, for example, when speaking of Asians refer to them as such; when speaking of themselves and Asians they use the term 'black'; and when speaking only of themselves do not see themselves as a sub-group of 'black' but as the black community. Race egalitarians and the media generally use a doublespeak in which Asians come to be and cease to be 'black' within a single sentence (pick up virtually any document on race for an example).

Another version of this patronising doublespeak occurs when local authority job advertisements proclaim a desire to attract applications from 'black and other ethnic minorities' or 'black and Asian people'. That in each case the second half of these invitations is very definitely secondary, an irritating addition, is clear from the fact that regardless of how often such words are used their order always follow strict precedence. Rare indeed in these contexts would a statement be made in terms of 'all ethnic minorities including black people'. And to expect a phrase such as 'Asian and black' might not seem unreasonable given our larger numbers or even the convention of alphabetical precedence, let alone the variety normal in the use of language; but it is an expectation which will invariably be disappointed for it misses the political nature of such formulae.

When added to this that an institution as central to public opinion formation as the BBC decides that the term 'black or Asian' is too cumbersome and that for the sake of editorial simplicity programme makers have the right to abbreviate that term to 'black', what are the Asians in Britain supposed to conclude about their significance as a community in Britain? What is the message that is being sent out to them?

As anyone knows, constantly being described as an appendix or as an afterthought erodes people's sense of worth so that they come to believe that they are perhaps as secondary or inferior as the benevolent authorities and the media imply. Whether it is for editorial or more worthy reasons the effect is the same: the imposition of a professional-political consensus on the Asian community formed by those largely outside it and dating from a time when Asians as a community were barely participants in debates on race.

It will be said that it is difficult to know what Asians think on these issues because they themselves are divided on it. Yet — and this speaks louder than any words — no one has attempted to establish what Asian grass-roots thinking is on this particular issue. (If any reader believes me to be mistaken here I sincerely would like to hear from them.) And is that not racist? Is it not comparable to, say, a local authority not bothering to find out whether its services are meeting the needs of its ethnically changing population instead of just assuming that they must do?

It is time the experts came to respect the principle of ethnic self-definition; or explain why it is not integral to race equality.

Source: *Equal Opportunities Review*, no 19, May/June 1988. For a fuller exposition of this argument and a response see Modood 1988b and Mason 1990 respectively; also Modood 1992d.

5

The Cricket Test:
a note to Mr Tebbit

Norman Tebbit's 'cricket test' for immigrant groups has been almost univer-sally condemned as a highly inappropriate and dangerous analogy. The suggestion that newly settled ethnic minorities won't cheer British sport teams seems ludicrous in the light of the levels of achievement by African-Caribbeans on behalf of Britain in not just cricket but football, athletics, boxing, judo and so on. While Asians cannot claim to match such a level of excellence it certainly is not on grounds of loyalty. In any case, support for teams (where I for one already find too much nationalism and male adolescent tribalism) is hardly a test of disloyal subjects.

Going beyond Mr Tebbit's mischievous and damaging remarks I would like to acknowledge that there is a serious issue about Britishness which needs to be addressed. Many young Asian people — especially if they have visited the country of their parents and grandparents — know how thoroughly they are a product of British society, outside of which they would be lost. Yet they do not, indeed cannot, glory in their Britishness for what, after all, is their status here? How can they when they are constantly told, not least by the Tebbits of this country, that they are not really British, that they do not belong here, that they must become indifferent to and preferably reject all that derives from their parents? You cannot treat a group of people as inferiors who are last to be hired and first to be fired, whose health, social services and even physical security needs are deemed unimportant on the grounds that they are immigrants, and at the same time expect a development in them of a confident sense of belonging to this country. When the experience of Asian people is that their right to be here remains an open political question and that success, requiring conformity, depends upon denying important parts of themselves, the embrace of Britishness is fraught with pain. What is the point of claiming to be as British as the next person when so few will accept the claim?

Of course there is a problem about British identity and non-white people in this country, but the single biggest cause is white racism. No one has a right to lecture Asians and others about lack of integration who is not actively challenging racism, for to do so is simply to stoke white and non-white fears. It is to create ethnic minority expectations which when dashed, as they will be, by white people will lead to more bitterness and sharper racial divisions.

Britain, having historically developed out of conquest and being comprised of several unequal nations, is familiar with nuanced identities where belonging to Britain is qualified by an important sense of, for example, a Welshness or a Scottishness. The Jews have rather successfully fitted into this pattern. Many states have been able to allow yet more complex national identities without compromising their national or political unity. Americans and Canadians, for example, are no less patriotic, even nationalistic, than anyone else but are not ashamed to proclaim and allow others to proclaim their ethnic diversity and immigrant origins. Many Americans glory in their hyphenated national identities and candidates for the highest political offices are publicly advertised as being Irish-American, Greek-American, African-American and so on. No one takes such community affiliations to be divisive or disloyal, for such communities and what they have brought into the country with them are seen to be a part of the national life. America's experience of large-scale immigration has been that incoming groups are more likely to become self-confident participants and adapt in their own way if they do not feel they are being compelled to conform to an allegedly superior culture, and if they are able to put their roots down as distinctive communities.

Indeed, this is a direction that British post-war immigration has also been taking, though in our case the facts of social change are ahead of national consciousness. Waking up to change and catching up with the facts can be a difficult experience, but it is what the country needs to do. While I do not think that all the current trends amongst ethnic minority communities — such as the neglect of English language amongst some groups — are for their own or Britain's long term good. Yet if we care for social harmony and national unity, the priority must be to dismantle the legacy of imperial racism and to develop forms of Britishness that go beyond a narrow nationalism. What we don't need are facile tests of loyalty that reinforce the social divisions they are supposed to eliminate.

Source: *New Life*, 4 May 1990

The ethnicity paradox

6

Beyond Racial Dualism: the case of the Indian economic success

In many countries 'minorities' means groups with advantageous social positions. Sometimes this implies conquering or political elites, as in several countries in Africa, not least South Africa. Often it is to talk of groups who enjoy little or no political power but derive their social position from economic or educational advantage. In European and colonial contexts one thinks of the Jews, the Chinese and Indians. India, however, is perhaps the most enduring example of where to be a small minority, the smaller the better, is to be economically and educationally better off than the majority, and where this is achieved in the absence of or before acquiring political power. While mass-minorities like the untouchables and Muslims suffer below-average conditions, many minorities that barely register 1% or 2% of the populations they reside amongst do rather well. Witness the success of minority faiths such as the Parsis and the Jains, of Muslim minority sects such as the Memons, the Bhoras and the Ismailis, and of the Gujarati Hindu sub-castes such as the Shahs, Lohanas and the Patels in the commercial and professional life of Bombay. This is achieved through the transmission of historically acquired and collectively tended group advantage, usually the exploitation of some socio-economic niche by means of an on-going community network and preferential treatment for members.

The subordination of certain minorities in Western societies has been such that 'minorities' here has come to have almost the opposite meaning. Of course, in the last century or so in America new minorities formed through immigration have, while maintaining a difference, flourished economically and made an important contribution to the national economy. These groups, mainly from the poorer or unstable parts of Europe, have however been white, and so it seemed for a long time that the principal social determinant was not

27

minority group membership but exclusion by colour and race. In recent years this picture has been complicated by the above average educational-economic profile of some non-white groups such as Japanese, Chinese, Koreans, Indians (South Asians), West Indians, Cubans and some, though not most other Spanish-speaking immigrant groups. Something similar is true of Canada and Australia. Nevertheless, the long historical experience of white racism and the knowledge of its contemporary existence in Britain have, I would suggest, led British race relations thinking to be over-influenced by the following set of assumptions:

1. Being white or not is the single most crucial factor in determining the sociological profile of any non-white group in contemporary Britain, dwarfing class, employment, capital assets, skills, gender, ethnicity, religion, education, family, geography and so on, all of which will be secondary in the sense that race determines each of these factors more than they determine race or each other in the total sociological outcome. Hence the sociology of any of the new ethnic minorities flows in its general outlines from this fundamental racial divide.

2. Until racial prejudice and discrimination in all its forms is eliminated, although some non-white individuals will be allowed to succeed, all non-white groups will share a below-average socio-economic profile: they will form a racial under-class.

3. The only way 'Black' people can improve their condition as a group is through political militancy and/or substantial state action; they are, therefore, a natural ally and integral component of left-wing movements.

I shall call this set of assumptions *racial dualism*, though the term only explicitly refers to the first of the set, for that is the key assumption and one from which the other two follow. The value of these assumptions is that they locate the phenomenon of race, including some of the most intractable forms of inequality, squarely within socio-political studies and policy frameworks. Yet the assumptions are not beyond criticism. By focusing on colour they suggest a concept of race which is considerably narrower than that embodied in the 1976 Race Relations Act and which too intimately links racial discrimination with socio-economic disadvantage. I do not here wish to engage directly with these assumptions, but would like to suggest some of their limitations by drawing attention to the evidence of an economic development which, if confirmed by further research, seriously challenges the over-generalised nature of the assumptions.

Racial Dualism and Asians

I have elsewhere presented and discussed two other important counter-examples to racial dualism which need to be borne in mind, to appreciate fully the challenge that Asians pose to racial dualism in the 1990s. The major one is the Muslim anger over Salman Rushdie's *The Satanic Verses*. The derogatory language and sexual imagery used in that novel to lampoon the Prophet Muhammad and his wives, reviving memories of Christian hate literature against Islam, is found deeply offensive by most Muslims, particularly by working class Asian Muslims who undertook a forceful campaign to have the novel withdrawn, created a race relations crisis that is barely intelligible within British anti-racist perspectives (Modood, 1990b). Four points are worth highlighting. Race theorists were unable to explain why this most socially deprived and racially harassed group should bear deprivation and harassment and yet explode in anger on an issue of religious honour. Second, the initial failure of the anti-racists and the media to register the issue suggests that dualistic antennae are not sensitive to ethnic minority concerns or outlooks. Third, the blend of anti-Muslim prejudice and colour-racism in the hysterical over-reaction to the anti-*Satanic Verses* demonstrators brought to the surface a highly specific form of cultural racism that the simplicities of racial dualism were of no assistance in opposing. Finally, Muslims neither looked to nor received any form of 'black' solidarity and many in 'black' politics dismissed Muslim anger as, in the words of Paul Boateng MP., having nothing to do with 'the black discourse' (Kramer, 1991:75). (Some, predominantly white, Christians were the only group to express any sympathy).

I have also drawn attention to how the concept of Black is harmful to Asians and is a form of political identity that most Asians do not accept as their primary public identity (Modood, 1988b). I cannot here rehearse the argument but if one single remark captures it, it is Yasmin Alibhai's contention that when most Asians hear the word 'black', they are unlikely to think of themselves and so many fail to apply for jobs where advertisements specifically welcome black people (BBC Radio 1988). It is not surprising, therefore, that in 1988 some Asians decided that an anti-racism that was so out of touch with or defiant of basic Asian community feelings had to be challenged. The year began with the National Association of Asian Probation Staff boycotting the Home Office staff ethnic monitoring exercise because it classified Asians as a sub-division of Black, and was followed by an on-going debate in the minority press, especially in *New Life, Asian Herald* and the African-Caribbean *Voice*, with overspills into the national media (Modood 1988a, Roy 1988, Uppal 1988, Kogbara 1988, BBC TV 1988). This critique bore fruit when in December of that year the Commission for Racial Equality (CRE) decided to cease to recommend that people of Asian origins be classified as Black (CRE, 1988b), and in the following month the Office of Population Censuses and Surveys announced that it was proceeding to the next stage in the ethnic question trials for the 1991 Census with the same categories as the CRE. The significance of these administrative decisions is perhaps an open question: were they just petty terminological changes or did they mark an important milestone in the philosophy of race relations? The CRE, which was disinclined to read too much into them, was told by a *New Statesman and Society* editorial that it 'should be publicising its decision with confidence instead of weakly whispering out an important decision, almost hoping nobody will notice' (23 December 1988). Phillip Nanton has argued that 'these attempts to capture an acceptable ethnic categorisation suggest that a fundamental change has taken place in the definition of ethnicity for ethnic categories can no longer be regarded as 'given' but are open to interest group pressure and negotiation (Nanton 1989:556). I would go further, but I will reserve my comment till I present the counter-example that is the subject of this article.

While some would now acknowledge that the concept of Black is in retreat it could still be argued that both of my examples, being concerned with inter-subjective identities, are only about tinkering with the 'superstructure' and do not get a grip on the 'material base'; and that it is only developments within that material base which determine the pertinence of the theory and practice of racial dualism. It is with this background of debate about what race means in Britain today that I wish to discuss the economic and employ-ment profile of the Indian community. The evidence here is limited and to some extent contradictory but I would like to sketch out an argument which I believe constitutes at least an important hypothesis about Indians which is worth consideration, and which if true has important implications for racial dualism.

Indians in Britain

According to the most reliable estimate there are about 800,000 people in Great Britain who are of Indian origin (Haskey, 1990). While they form only 1.4% of the population, they are easily the most numerous of the nine non-white groups in the Labour Force survey and indeed amount to almost a third (33%) of all non-white people in the country (West-Indians at 19% and Pakistanis at 17% are the two next largest groups). They have for some years had an economic-educational profile which is much closer to that of the white majority than of the other non-white groups and may now have reached a point where, taken in the round, their performance is, or can be expected to shortly be, equal to that of white people. Before we look at these figures, however, I would like to give some brief indication of the composition of the group. There are many ways of distinguishing between Indians, and while some quite elaborate typologies have been developed on the basis of region of origin, language, religion and caste,[1] I would like to suggest the following simple sub-divisions, for they identify recognisable communities in terms of origins and settlement as well as in terms of class, skills and capital; that is to say, the basic determinants, other than race, of their point of entry and development in the British economy.

1. The single largest group, amounting to perhaps 40%, is the Punjabis, mainly Sikhs,[2] from peasant-farmer origins. They are the longest settled of the major South Asian groups in Britain, with family unification and cessation of remittances to India having taken place in the 1960s and

1970s (and to an extent which is not yet so with Pakistanis and Bangladeshis) (Ballard and Vellins 1985: 262; Ballard 1990). They have established communities particularly in Gravesend, in outer West London, especially Southall, and the West Midlands, especially Birmingham and Coventry. They came with a very small college-educated class but my guess is that in terms of income and property they now probably nearly approximately to the class profile of Britain, at least in respect of males and those under 30 years old.[3]

2. Far less numerous are the East Africans (about two-thirds Gujaratis to one-third Punjabis) who came in the late 1960s and 1970s mainly as refugee families, rather than as most other South Asian groups who came as male economic migrants and left the option open as to whether they would wish to make Britain a land of settlement. (Settlement was usually hastened if not precipitated by restrictive immigration laws passed in panic). They are not usually numerous enough to be large communities, Leicester and the Wembley/Harrow area of outer North-West London being the major exceptions. They were predominantly urban, professional-commercial, predominantly middle class and wealthy in East Africa, and though many lost much of their capital and income in the expulsion from that region, through education, skills, experience, hard work, family and community network, international trading contacts and so on, they have gone a long way in recreating the class composition they enjoyed in East Africa. The Gujaratis are mainly Hindu but include some Muslims, mainly Shia minorities like Ismailis, some of whom are amongst the most wealthy of all Indians.

3. Urban professionals from several parts of India who came as students or newly qualified professionals in medicine, law, accountancy, engineering, etc. They are too small in number to form local communities; in so far as they are active members of any Asian community it is through sharing the community life of the first and/or second groups.

4. Those who came directly from Gujarat (as opposed to via E. Africa) are mainly Hindus settled in the Midlands, with a similar skills background and current profile to the Punjabis. About a third of rural Gujaratis are, however, Sunni (i.e. the majority sect) Muslims and like their co-religionists in this country from Pakistan and Bangladesh they came poor in education, relevant skills and capital. They are particularly settled in the North, in such Lancashire towns as Blackburn, Bolton and Preston, as well as Leicester. While their educational-economic position may have improved over the years it is not at all comparable to the other Indian groups but is, in my view, similar to that of the Pakistanis and Bangladeshis, a contrast which will become clearer as I proceed.

It ought to be said that there is very little direct evidence to suggest that the educational-economic profile of the rural Muslim Gujaratis is like that of other South Asian Muslims rather than that of the other Indian groups. For evidence is rarely available which distinguishes between different Indian groups. I believe, however, that a comparative study of the position of Indians where rural Muslim Gujaratis are preponderant (eg Blackburn) with areas where East Africans are preponderant (eg Wembley) would support my claim. Table 1 is offered as one of the few pieces of direct evidence. It will be seen that the Hindu and Sikh male earnings are higher than for Indians and African Asian men as a group. I infer that the male Indian and African Asian figure is depressed by the 15-20% of Indians and Africans Asians who are Muslim (Smith 1976:12). Indeed, the assumption that 20% of the Indian and East African men are Muslims gives them an average gross earning which is the same as for Pakistanis. This is an earnings differential of about 9%. It will also be seen that the earnings differential between Muslim and non-Muslim women is almost double that figure, though some of the evidence for this is bracketed because of the smallness of the sample of Muslim women. This last is due to the fact that relatively few Muslim women are in paid employment. That, however, means that there is an even more substantial income differential when measured by households. Moreover, when we bear in mind that Muslim couples have more children, and also take into account rent, income generated from savings made possible by larger disposable incomes and smaller remittances abroad, not to mention the capital growth likely with more desirable residential and commercial property, we begin to get a measure of the difference in the economic profile between Muslims and other Asians. The gap is likely to be quite a bit greater than it was in 1982, the date of the data in Table 1, though it also has to be said that the pooling together of resources through joint family living (the sharing of a house and other

Table 1: ASIANS: FULL-TIME EMPLOYEES' GROSS EARNINGS (1982)

Median Weekly Pay

	MEN	WOMEN
All Asians	110.70	73.00
Indian	115.40	72.80
Pakistani	106.20	(64.30)
Bangladeshi	88.50	(43.80)
African Asian	114.20	76.80
Muslim	103.30	(67.10)
Hindu	117.20	79.60
Sikh	116.10	68.90

Source: Colin Brown, *Black and White Britain*, Third PSI Survey (1984), Table 11, p.216.

assets by two or more brothers and their families) and kinship networks creates forms of collective income and capital not easy to measure by the methods of British social surveys.

Nevertheless, if Sunni Muslim, Shia Muslim, Hindu, Sikh were to be used as sociological and equality monitoring categories, they would reveal that by most socio-economic measures there is a major divide between Sunni Muslims on the one hand and the other Asians, and that this divide is as great as between Asian and whites, or between Asians and blacks. For these reasons one ought to bracket off the rural Muslim Gujaratis from the rest of British Indians for the purpose of this analysis; not because they are any less Indian than the other groups, but because they are an exception to the Indian socio-economic pattern which holds for the overwhelming majority of Indians. As most of the data that I adduce is not divisible into Indian sub-groups, I ask the reader to bear in mind that the presence of the rural Muslim Gujaratis in the holistic Indian figures has the effects of depressing Indian aggregates and obscuring the scale of the educational-economic achievement of the other Indian groups.

Indians in the economy

Tables 2 and 3 show that more or less consistently throughout the 1980s Indian men, particularly Hindus and Sikhs, in sharp contradistinction to other non-white groups, had unemployment rates that were about the same as those of white people. Table 4 illustrates that at least *prima facie* the position at the top is no less comparatively healthy than at the bottom. This table, which like some of the other Labour Force Survey data used here, is based on averaging the latest three years' data in order to increase reliability (at a small risk of under-estimating dynamic processes) and is broadly consistent with the data of the early 1980s. It shows that out of the main identifiable male groups Indians feature most prominently in non-manual occupations; moreover, their advantage over the white group is greater when one looks at the upper end of this spectrum (42% of Indians in the managerial and professional (M&P) category compared to 35% of whites). The difference between Indian and other ethnic minority men is therefore not only considerable but is greater than between the latter and white men. The contrasts between groups of women is not so dramatic but, on the other hand, the figures for women do not suggest any racial disparities between those in work though they further remind us that much smaller number of Pakistanis and Bangladeshis (and rural Muslim Gujaratis) are in work compared to all other women.

One's first reaction to table 4, despite its consistency with previous data, is to refuse to believe it. For the figures are so contrary to the evidence of one's eyes, namely that the major professions and management tiers are not brimming with Indians. The figures only accord with experience when one recognises that the M&P category includes all forms of self-employment. For the fact, as evidenced by Table 5, that a large portion of Indians are in self-employment is supported by experience. Hence it turns out that while

Table 2: UNEMPLOYMENT RATE BY SEX AND ETHNIC GROUP (1982)

	MEN	WOMEN
White	13	10
West Indian	25	16
Asian	20	20
Indian	14	18
Pakistani	29	(28)
Bangladeshi	29	(52)
African Asian	17	21
Muslim	27	31
Hindu	14	22
Sikh	14	22

Source: Colin Brown, *Black and White Britain*, (1984), Table 83, p.189.

Table 3: TRENDS IN MALE UNEMPLOYMENT RATES BY ETHNIC ORIGIN
Spring 1984 to Spring 1991

	1984	1985	1986	1987	1988	1989	1990	199
All origin	11.9	11.5	11.5	11.0	8.9	7.2	6.9	9.1
White	11.4	11.0	11.1	10.7	8.6	6.9	7	9.0
Ethnic minority group	22.1	21.6	20.5	17.4	14.2	12.7	11	16.0
of whom:								
West Indian/Guyanese	30	24	26	21	18	15.1	13	18
Indian	13	19	16	10	11	9.9	8	12
Pakistani/Bangladeshi	33	28	27	30	24	21.4	15	25
All other origins	19	18	17	15	9	7.9	22	14

Source: Labour Force Survey, *Employment Gazette*, March 1990, Table 8, p.133, and April 1990, Table 23, p.210; April 1991, Table 17, p.191; and April 1992, Table 20, p.168.

34

15% of employed white men are in self-employment (leaving a remainder of 20% in the remaining M&P category), 27% of Indian men are in self-employment (leaving a nevertheless significant 15% in the remaining M&P category compared to only 6% of West Indians and 4% of Pakistanis and Bangladeshis). Thus, whatever the evidence of our eyes, if Labour Force Survey data are to be taken at face value, it is not the case, as it clearly is for Pakistanis and Bangladeshis, that Indians are prominent in the top category only because of self-employment.

Nevertheless, given the importance of self-employment to the Indian socio-economic profile, I think we need briefly to examine more closely the assumption that Indian self-employment is not economically the equivalent of that of whites and so the presence of a large Indian figure in the M&P category is not an accurate reflection of the Indian economic standing in the country. Academic researchers, most notably the ESRC funded project of 1978-82, have for example taken the view that Asian-owned shops are not viable forms of economic success and concluded that as such shops are a major form of Indian self-employment then the rosy statistics disguise the existence of an under-class, a lumpenbourgeoisie, that lies behind them (McEvoy et al 1982; Aldrich et al 1984). Now, it is very likely true that the majority of Indian self-employment is in retail: general and 'ethnic' groceries, newsagents and confectionaries, sub post-offices, off-licences, take-away food, video rentals and supermarkets primarily, but also haberdashery, clothes and, in some areas, jewellery. I find, however, the view that such enterprise is an economic dead-end totally counter to personal experience, which is that Indian-owned shops usually expand (eg if they start off as groceries, they build on an off-licence section); if they are sold, which is the exception, it is usually to another Indian or Asian aspiring entrepreneur; proprietors are usually looking for neighbouring sites to buy up and install a relative in; Asians often leave paid employment (including graduates in professional jobs) to take up self-employment but the reverse is rare; if Asians sell up it is usually to move 'upmarket'. As far as I know no statistics exist to record all this, so all I can offer is personal witness (though see Patel 1985; Menski 1983) and note that academic studies reach what I regard as counter-to-experience conclusions because they usually assume some or all of the following:

- studies based on 'inner city' wards are an adequate sample of all Asian retailers;

- if an Asian buys a failing white-owned business he can do no better (even though he will open longer hours, stock wider range of items and use his cultural knowledge to meet demand and use sources of supply that his predecessor did not know existed);

35

Table 4: Employment by broad occupation, ethnic origin and sex: spring 1986 to 1988 (Source: Labour Force Survey, *Employment Gazette*, March 1990, Table 5, p.130.

	All origins‡	White	Ethnic minority groups	of whom: West Indian/ Guyanese	Indian	Pakistani/ Bangladeshi	All other origins§
All							
All (thousands = 100 per cent)	23,919	22,861	873	217	307	100	249
All non-manual occupations	55	55	54	45	58	41	61
Managerial and professional	31	31	31	22	34	28	37
Clerical and related	16	16	15	18	16	*	16
Other non-manual	8	8	7	6	7	*	8
All manual occupations	45	45	46	55	42	59	39
Craft and similar	16	16	15	16	16	16	11
General labourers	1	1	1	*	*	*	*
Other manual	28	28	31	37	25	41	28
Males							
All (thousands = 100 per cent)	13,754	13,127	522	108	185	82	147
All non-manual occupations	47	47	46	28	54	36	56
Managerial and professional	35	35	33	15	42	27	40
Clerical and related	5	5	6	*	7	*	7
Other non-manual	6	6	7	*	6	*	8
All manual occupations	53	53	54	72	46	64	44
Craft and similar	25	25	20	29	19	17	15
General labourers	1	1	*	*	*	*	*
Other manual	27	27	33	40	26	45	28
Females							
All (thousands = 100 per cent)	10,165	9,734	351	108	122	18	103
All non-manual occupations	66	66	64	62	62	65	68
Managerial and professional	26	26	28	29	23	*	32
Clerical and related	30	30	29	28	30	*	29
Other non-manual	10	10	7	*	9	*	*
All manual occupations	34	34	36	38	38	*	32
Crafts and similar	4	4	7	*	12	*	*
General labourers	0	0	*	*	*	*	*
Other manual	30	30	28	34	24	*	27

* Less than 10 000 in cell, estimate not shown.
‡ Excluding those on Government schemes.
† Includes those who did not state origin
§ Includes those of Mixed origin.

36

Table 5: Economic status of people in employment by sex and origin; average: spring 1986 to 1988. (Source: Labour Force Survey, *Employment Gazette*; March 1990, Table 3, p.129.)

Persons of working age (16 to 59/64)

Great Britain
Per cent

	All origins†	White	Ethnic minority groups	of whom: West Indian/ Guyanese	Indian	Pakistani/ Bangladeshi	All other origins‡
All							
Economically active (thousands)	*26,435*	*25,161*	*1,068*	*274*	*360*	*142*	*292*
In employment (thousands= 100 per cent)	*23,736*	*22,664*	*889*	*222*	*310*	*104*	*252*
of which: Employees§	86	86	82	90	77	74	83
Full-time	68	68	69	76	66	65	67
Part-time	18	19	13	14	11	*	16
Self-employed	12	12	16	6	21	22	15
On Government schemes	2	2	3	*	*	*	*
Males							
Economically active (thousands)	*15,427*	*14,667*	*642*	*143*	*213*	*115*	*171*
In employment (thousands= 100 per cent)	*13,814*	*13,177*	*531*	*112*	*187*	*84*	*148*
of which: Employees§	82	83	77	86	71	75	80
Full-time	80	80	73	83	68	69	75
Part-time	3	3	4	*	*	*	*
Self-employed	15	15	20	9	27	23	19
On Government schemes	2	2	3	*	*	*	*
Females							
Economically active (thousands)	*11,008*	*10,494*	*426*	*130*	*147*	*27*	*121*
In employment (thousands= 100 per cent)	*9,923*	*9,487*	*358*	*110*	*124*	*20*	*104*
of which: Employees§	91	92	88	94	86	70	88
Full-time	52	51	62	69	63	48	55
Part-time	40	40	26	25	23	*	32
Self-employed	7	7	9	*	12	*	9
On Government schemes	2	2	3	*	*	*	*

· Less than 10,000 in cell; estimate not shown
† Includes those wo did not state origin
‡ Includes those of mixed orgin
§ Excluding those of Government schemes. The full-time classification is based on respondents self-assessment.

37

- if an Asian business closes or is sold it means that it is not profitable (in fact it is just as or more likely that the owner has saved enough to move 'upmarket');

- long unpaid unsocial hours put in by members of the family are interpreted as evidence of long term unprofitability not as the utilisation of unproductive leisure time to secure current family income and a long-term asset.

On the basis of assumptions such as these, researchers have concluded that the small Asian-owned shop is an economic dead-end in the same period of time that the subjects of their study have expanded turnover, outlets, range of products and capital value, and it is estimated that Asians (primarily Indians) by the end of the 1980s owned not much under 50% of the independent retail outlets in the country as a whole, with a much higher proportion in the principal urban areas (Parekh 1990:1). I find it difficult to accept this 50% figure but, nevertheless, against the research consensus I continue to hold the lay view that the despised corner shop has played an important part in the Indian success.[4] Though of course Indians are playing a notable part through ownership in other sectors of the economy, most notably in cash and carry, textiles, property, restaurants, hotels, import-export and increasingly, in manufacture.

It is now estimated that 300 of the 18,000 millionaires in Britain are Asian (Skeel, 1990: 60). While there are no data on how many of these Asians are Indian, a glance at the names and biographies of the top fifty shows them to be predominantly Hindus and Indians.[5] If one estimated that three quarters of the 300 were Indians and nearly all of the remaining 17,700 white, it would mean that Indians were represented as millionaires in the same proportion as whites (0.03%). If one were to confine the comparison to those who became millionaires post-1975, the Indian success would be overwhelming. Quantity of millionaires of course is not by itself a satisfactory criterion of economic success of a community but I believe that the interedependent nature of the Indian community and the estimated 5 billion purchasing power of Asians suggests a distribution of success at all levels and not just at the very top. Indeed, it is remarkable how many Indian millionaires began with the humble corner shop. In any case, the pattern of evidence suggests that amongst Asian businesses the Indian ones are larger than those of others (Robinson and Flintoff, 1982; Employment Institute 1990:4)[6].

We should not forget that the Indian presence in the M&P category is by no means confined to commerce or self-employment. Most professions do not keep records of the ethnic origin of their members, and even those who do, do not usually use the category 'Indian'. But it is worth looking at some of the available data. A large proportion of the 26% of the doctors in NHS hospitals in 1988 who were not born in the EC, as well as of the 16% of GPs born in South Asia, are likely to be Indian (as of course will be some who were born in the UK) (Department of Health 1989a and 1989b). This will be so by a factor which exceeds by several times the 1.4% that Indians form of the population. The same will also be true of the 9.4% of the British Asians who entered medical school in 1986 (McManus *et al* 1989: 726); and the same will be true of the 2.5% of all barristers and 5% of all barrister pupils in 1988 who are Asians (Smith 1989: 9 and 12)[7]; of the 5.5% of the Law Society's student enrolment in 1989 who were Asian (Law Society 1989); and of the 7% of the Asians who received training contracts in 1989 from four of the largest and most prestigious firms of chartered accountants (CRE 1990a). Mahesh Kumar, who founded the Asian City Club because of the need felt for mutual support by the few Asians in the City at that time, now speaks of the City as 'infested with Asians' (Wahhab, 1990) and one of the best journalists on Asian affairs believes 'bright young Asians are pouring out of Oxbridge into the business world' (Roy, 1990: 16).

Of course for every profession in which Indians are notably present there are several in which they are under-represented and this is no doubt so in those professions and firms where there is no ethnic monitoring data as well as in the public sector where monitoring is now undertaken. This ought not to be understated. Yet with the demographic trough and severe shortages of supply at higher skill levels, Indian men and women, who for many years have enjoyed a greater relative share of university places than whites (Vellins 1982; Ballard and Vellins 1985; Tanna 1990: 356 for further evidence that most of Asian university students are Indians), and are increasingly successfully targeting the most prestigious institutions;[8] and with the percentage of Indian men under 30 in P&M work twice as high as among their white counterparts (Field 1987: 119), this group must stand the greatest chance of breaking out from the strongholds and gaining entry into most areas of British commercial and professional life. Indeed, whether Indians achieve that breakthrough or not will be a major test of how 'colour-blind' these areas of British life are.

Some challenges to racial dualism

While there is too little evidence in this area of study to make dogmatic statements and while therefore my suggestion of an Indian economic success stands more as a hypothesis than as an incontrovertible fact, I hope I have made enough of a case to offer a further counter-example to the assumptions of racial dualism.[9] My argument is so open to misunderstanding that at least three other qualifications are essential. Firstly, I am not arguing that there is an elite of Indians who are doing nicely-thank-you (Robinson 1988). Such elites exist in most ethnic minority groups; my argument is about Indians *as a group* compared to other groups. Nor is my argument that Indians are the only minority group which is making relative improvements and has a growing middle-class portion: this is true of all groups, but none of the more significantly sized groups for whom data is available can match the Indian starting point and scale of improvement. (West Africans, for example, are a group for whom very little data is available, but who may be in a comparable position to Indians.) The advantage of citing the case of Indians is precisely so that my example is not marginal: because of their number, Indians are central to what it means to be 'black' in Britain.

Thirdly and most importantly, nothing that I have said should lead one to believe that Indians do not suffer colour prejudice and racial discrimination, or will soon cease to suffer, or suffer less than other groups. For the truth is exactly the opposite. Michael Banton has argued that in the early years of ex-empire immigration 'the English seemed to display more hostility towards the West Indians because they sought a greater degree of acceptance than the English wished to accord; in more recent times there seems to have been more hostility towards Asians because they are insufficiently inclined to adopt English ways' (Banton, 1979: 242). This was indeed the experience of Dervla Murphy in her sojourns in Bradford and Birmingham (Murphy 1987). A 1989 European Community survey found that Asians were the most disliked group in Britain (*Today*, 14 March 1990), a finding which was confirmed by a Scottish-Nigerian writer on race in his travels around Britain (Maja-Pearce, 1990: 72).[10] The last two temperature readings were taken when the Rushdie Affair was still alive and 'Asian' for many respondents must have meant Asian Muslims. Yet, just as Indians are often harassed and taunted as 'Pakis', all South Asian groups have suffered from the fall-out from the Rushdie affair and it is to be expected that at least for some time, at the level of prejudice and acts of racism, these groups will continue to blur into each other. Moreover, as we all know, the threat of competition, as well as resentment and envy of successful groups, are (as E. African Indians are only too painfully aware) some of the primary causes of racial prejudice and restrictive practices. It is likely that these will increase unless other more conspicuous and noisier scapegoats are found. In any case when it comes to face-to-face discrimination, for example in seeking accommodation or employment, all the evidence is that colour is still the decisive factor (Brown and Gay: 1985; CRE 1990b; Foyster *et al* 1990). CRE investigations into the selection of students at St George's Medical School, into offers of training contracts with the leading chartered accountancy firms and into the graduate labour market give ample evidence of the differential success rates between *prima facie* equally qualified white and ethnic minority persons, including Indians (Commission for Racial Equality 1987; 1988; Brennan and McGeevor 1990). Indeed, the large Indian presence in small business is itself partly a product of racial discrimination: the experience of discrimination in getting jobs and promotions leads many to self-employment as a means of social mobility or even survival, for it seems to be easier to win custom from those who will not give one employment (Ballard 1989: 213-5).

I have cited the example of Indian success because I believe it poses a triple challenge to racial dualism. The first is simply the recognition of the fact itself and the posing of the question why it has not been noticed and investigated. For while it has been a remarkably quick phenomenon (pre-First World War Jewish immigration probably took longer to achieve the same), it has not happened overnight. The trend has been visible from at least the early 1980s though it has been least visible to race researchers. Additionally, there are two major implications caused by the fact, if it should be confirmed, which will not be easy to harmonise with racial dualism. One is the unbuckling of the link between racial discrimination and socio-economic disadvantage. The assumptions that the nature of British society is such that racially discriminated groups must form a socio-economic under-class and that unity of these groups will harmonise with working class politics will begin to look awfully facile. A separating out of racial discrimination and disadvantage has often been the case in the past and is true with a wide variety of groups in USA today, not least the Japanese, Chinese, Indians and West Indians. Yet the possibility that not only individuals but groups can be, as it were, whites in achievement and blacks in discrimination is an idea which barely registers within the terms of racial dualism. It is certainly not an issue to which dualism can be expected to provide a reasoned policy strategy. To his credit, this question has been addressed by Malcolm Cross, the editor of *New Community*, the research journal of the Commission for Racial Equality. In a short yet significant journalistic piece, he argues:

> Asian pupils do better than whites and African-Caribbeans in terms of measured school performance, even allowing for school type and social class. This fact, and other evidence of 'success' makes it harder to sustain the argument that blanket racism is the prime cause of low performance (Cross, 1989: p.35).

The first thing that has to be said about the facts in question is that they do not exist: there is no such Asian success. What there is, as we have seen, is Indian success, while the situation of Pakistanis and especially Bangladeshis is on many counts worse than that of African-Caribbeans or any other group. Nevertheless, the statement that some non-white groups are succeeding such that there cannot be a simple linkage between racial discrimination and racial disadvantage is important, coming as it does not from a right-wing critic but from someone who for two decades has been in the mainstream of race relations sociology and has excellent social democratic credentials. The statement requires far deeper consideration than Cross was able to give it, not least about forms of political unity amongst discriminated groups.

If the second challenge, then, is to re-think the link between discrimination and disadvantage, the third goes even deeper, for it poses questions about the ends and means of racial equality and of what it is possible to achieve. The Indian success is not an accident, something which that community just stumbled across. While it could not be said to be planned or organised, and naturally depends upon the character and level of pre-migration skills and capital, it nevertheless is an example of a community style, of the operation of collective norms and values. I would characterise this community style as a strategy of putting family before self, of long hours of work and thrift, of creating new businesses and seeking academic and professional qualifica-

41

tions in excess of what white people think is adequate for themselves. In the manner of the Bombay minorities it consists on the one hand of expanding the economy through mutual self-help and, on the other hand, of competing for, and preparing one's children to compete for, 'meritocratic' careers by a drive for all available qualifications and forms of respectability and social distinction. Such a strategy may not dent racial discrimination but can compensate for it and perhaps enable one to rise above it in some contexts. Instead of channelling one's energy into eliminating racial discrimination it is a strategy of channelling one's energies to succeed despite discrimination. It is evidenced for example in the way that Indian students, by specialising in subjects and careers which have above average graduate salaries, compensate for the discrimination against them, and as a group probably have higher earnings than white graduates in at least the first few years after graduation (Dolton et al 1990: 51-52); Brennan and McGeevor 1990:61-65).

The emphasis is on outcomes rather than formal justice; the goal is success rather than equal treatment; 'getting on' rather than equitable shares. The challenge for a politicised racial dualism is, therefore, of ends and means. Can it accept such a circumspect approach in which anti-racism is not directly pursued? On the other hand, can it altogether dismiss what such an apolitical approach actually delivers? Group interest and principle should mutually inform each other but, as in for instance labourism and socialism, they can at times be out of joint and need to be reharmonised in the light of events. One needs in particular to be careful that the legitimising principles do not obscure or impede desirable social developments.

Race equality thinking consists of a number of different ideological strands. I have in mind ideological outlooks such as universalism, which emphasises uniformity of treatment; or social utilitarianism, which focuses on remedial state action to overcome racial disadvantage; or the anti-racism which is a dimension of class struggle; or the ethnic pluralism which emphasises the diversity of values, the cultural dimension of oppression and the non-political ways in which ethnic groups contribute to social outcomes including racial equality. Each of these is an important ingredient of egalitarian theory and practice but different times and situations will see different balances between them. With the possible exception of multi-cultural education, the balance in the 1980s has been in favour of universalism and social utilitarianism wrapped in a rhetoric of anti-racism, and a key expression of this mix has been the acceptance of the political term 'Black' into the mainstream.

It is here that the official retreat from the concept of Black is relevant, for in taking the decision that utilitarian and anti-racist perspectives are not decisive on the question of ethnic monitoring, that monitoring classifications should harmonise with people's self-perceptions, the CRE and OPCS have limited these perspectives in favour of the principles of ethnic pluralism and respect for ethnic identities. It may be that this is an intimation of a new balance amongst the competing and complementary strands of our concept of racial equality. It may be that the decision to cease officially to impose the term 'Black' upon people of South Asian origin will in retrospect be seen as marking the limit of the influence of militant racial dualism and the opening towards a new balance in the concept of racial equality.

As far as the Indian success is concerned, it is important to recognise it as a genuine achievement but also not to overlook the cost. For it is paid for by a high degree of self-denial and loss of self-development, by family discipline and the long hours of dull and often menial work on the part of parents, and the pressures on the young consequent on high parental expectations of academic success. All this in a context of racial prejudice and harassment, cultural adaptation and the inevitable fears on the part of the parents that they will 'lose' their children; while the young have to cope with cultural influences and attractions, family obligations and desire to seek acceptance in British society, that do not always lend themselves to easy or painless syntheses. Some of the psychic tensions are beginning to show and Bhikhu Parekh has said he believes that the 'bubble of Asian success' is about to burst as the family and kinship mutual help, the foundations of this success breaks down (Parekh 1990: 1-2). For my part, I think this prognosis assumes a rate of 'assimilation', the triumph of British ideas of self and family and happiness over Indian, that may be greater than is actually the case even among the young. My own speculation is that the Indian family and community structure will function long enough for Indians to reach and consolidate the above-average socio-economic positioning; its fate, thereafter, may primarily depend upon the extent to which the English allow Indians to be integrated into the class structure of this country or make them a marginal, if prosperous, caste. Like the Jews before them, the Indian family and kinship networks will last as long as Indians are not able to flourish without them.

The present ferment amongst Asian Muslims illustrates how the sense of being humiliated and marginalised enhances traditional forms of solidarity. It also suggests that British Asians can crudely be split into two groups: the achievers and the believers. As neither group understands itself in terms of or draws its strength from a colour solidarity, the theory and politics of racial dualism are faced with challenges which it does not have the flexibility to cope with. Yet racial discrimination will continue to shape the circumstances of these and other non-white groups. It is vital, therefore, that our race equality thinking not be bounded by the simplicities of dualism.

Notes

1. In addition to a very elaborate typology Robinson (1986) makes a distinction between South Asians and East Africans as the primary distinction between Asians: but this only works in towns like Blackburn where the large majority of Indians are rural Muslim Gujaratis and hence more like Pakistanis than the East Africans. The primary distinction in reality is between Sunni Muslims and everyone else.

2. Not always. Most Indian Punjabis in South Oxford for instance are Christians. With their lower-caste origins, their socio-economic profile is like the Pakistanis' rather than the Sikhs'.

3. The Punjabis are therefore a counter-example to the assertion that most black and Asian people experienced downward social mobility as a result of migration (Robinson 1990: 275). While Pakistanis and Bangladeshies are even clearer counter-examples, immigration to Britain enabled must Punjabi families to improve their standard of living and prospects in both the new and the old countries.

4. My scepticism may be unwarranted. Mars, the UK confectionary maker, has recently completed a comprehensive survey of fast-moving consumer goods outlets and concluded that 65% of independently owned shops in Britain are Asian-owned (the figure for the area ringed by the M25 in south-east England is 95%). Most significantly 78% of the independent retail sector is controlled by just one Indian group, East African Gujaratis (Merchant: 1991). For an example of how to sociologise in the face of overwhelming evidence against one's thesis, rather than simply admit one was wrong, see Cater and Jones, 1991. For evidence that Asian traders, most of whom bank with the High Street four, particularly Barclays, are going to be able to survive the BCCI collapse, see Fielding 1992. In this field, the sensationalism of journalists is proving to be less of a barrier to truth than the ideological bias of academic researchers.

5. Of the fifteen or so Asian millionaires that the Prime Minister, Mr Major, invited to the dinner to celebrate the first anniversary of his premiership, only one was non-Indian (*Sunday Telegraph*, 1 December 1991).

6. An important piece of supporting evidence for my argument about the poorer socio-economic situation of Sunni Muslim Asians compared to other Asians has recently emerged. Its importance lies in that it is a study of Bradford, an area which with its concentration of Muslims and their community networks, one would expect a high comparative Muslim performance (Rafiq, 1992).

7. I do not think it has been noted that Africans and African-Caribbeans are very strongly represented at the Bar (certainly in a greater proportion than whites or Indians). The non-whites are, of course, disproportionately in the less prestigious chambers.

8. For example, of Cambridge University's 1991 intake of British students 2.6% were Indians (compared to a student-age Indian population of 1.75%), while Pakistanis and Bangladeshis were only 0.3% and 0.2% respectively. Following on from note 4, it does seem, now that the data is finally being collected, that higher education may prove to be another area where race relations research theses may be defeated by the facts (Modood, forthcoming).

9. Since writing this paper I have come across the important finding that in Leicester Indians earn 20% less than whites (Duffy and Lincoln 1990). While I am not here able to evaluate this research I note that the comparison is not based on actual gross earnings but on basic gross earnings even though it was found that Indians did more

overtime and were twice as likely to do shift work and receive premiums. More significantly, the findings are seriously contrary to the New Earnings Survey (Leicester is found by Duffy and Lincoln to have average earnings of only 74% of what the survey gives as the East Midlands average) and its figures on social class are grossly inconsistent with the successive findings of the Labour Force Survey. Part of the problem may be in the fact that the Indian sample has a large under-representation of young men and has a disproportionate 'inner-city' weighting. For the contrary finding that ethnic minority graduates (amongst whom Indians feature largely) earn more than their white peers see Brennan and McGeever (1990): 61-65 and Dolton et al (1990): 51-52.

10. He writes: 'this obsessive hatred of people from the Indian sub-continent is parallelled in recent history by a well-known event in central Europe' (Maja-Pearce, 1990: 72). In fact, the finding of all the white attitude surveys over several decades is that self-assigned racial prejudice against Asians is higher, sometimes much higher, than against black people (e.g. Brown 1984:290; Jowell *et al* 1986: 150 and 164; Amin and Richardson 1992: 19-21).

Source: *Policy and Politics*, 19(3) July 1991.

7

Being Somebody and
Being Oppressed:
catching up with Jesse Jackson

'Say after me: I am somebody! Say it again: I AM SOMEBODY!'
—*Jesse Jackson*

The working class Asian Muslim anger over *The Satanic Verses* and the ensuing crisis constitutes one of the major events of British race relations. Yet, as the Iranian revolution was to the CIA and the invasion of the Falklands to British military intelligence, so Muslim anger has been to British anti-racism. It is barely intelligible, let alone predictable, within British anti-racist perspectives. Throughout the 1980s, of the nine non-white groups identified in the Labour Force Survey, Pakistanis and Bangladeshis have suffered the highest rates of unemployment, have the lowest number of educational qualifications and the highest profile in manual work; and this is true in each respect, not just for women but also for men, and not just for the middle-aged (the first generation) but also the young (see also East Birmingham Task Force 1989). The impact on them from immigration laws and rules has been the most adverse, they have the worst housing and suffer from the highest levels of attacks on person and property. If a racial underclass exists in Britain, here it is. Why should this most socially deprived and racially harassed group bear all this, and yet explode in anger on an issue of religious honour? Why should this explosion take place in Britain rather than France, West Germany or America where the numbers of Muslims are greater, hostility against them no less and their condition much worse in the two European countries? I submit that the fact that the available theories of race look like non-starters in answering such questions is a serious drawback to any claims to be interpreters of social reality in the Britain that we live in.

I have argued elsewhere that the events in question cannot be understood without some knowledge of the relevant ethnic history, the specially South Asian veneration of the Prophet, and the cultural rejection and insecurity experienced in Britain, as well as the more familiar pattern of racial discrimination and disadvantage (Modood 1990b). What is required, however, are not simply extra bits of information. The prior step is to reform those theoretical perspectives, based upon narrow concepts of race, which deny the intrinsic relevance of ethnicity and cultural histories to an understanding of race relations and to anti-racist strategies. For, on the one hand, inadequate conceptualisation can shut off lines of research and policy issues; on the other, information by itself does not deepen understanding or yield explanatory connections.

What is needed is a sociology that is able to connect a group's internal structure, values and understanding of itself, commonly understood as ethnicity, with how that group is categorised and treated as a subordinate race within a wider society. These elements, ethnicity and race, or as I prefer it, a group's mode of being and the mode of oppression it suffers, are familiar elements to the sociologists who provide the current frameworks for anti-racist policies, yet they are unable fruitfully to relate the two and thereby assume that ethnicity is of lesser importance. This leads not only to inadequate explanations, and sometimes non-explanations, of events. It leads to suppression of group identities and undermines a vital ingredient in anti-racist strategies, group pride.[1]

British race sociology and not being somebody

John Rex, who has been of some influence in shaping British race sociology, looks on ethnicity as no more a form of group self-understanding than are physical characteristics. While he shares the view that a race is an externally imposed identity on a group of people who may not have thought of themselves as being a group, he holds that ethnicity also is in this category. In the way that the categorisations of a dominant group can create a quasi-group out of those who share similar physical appearance, so similarly an ethnic group is a quasi-group based on what are perceived by non-members to be distinctive cultural characteristics of a given population. Rex makes an explicit analogy with Marx's distinction between a 'class-in-itself' and 'class-for-itself'. The existence of a racial or ethnic quasi-group depends upon its treatment by a dominant group or its socio-economic location. The quasi-group becomes a group in the full sense when it uses its racial and/or cultural and/or whatever other resources are available to develop forms of organisation to defend or promote its interests against the other group(s) (Rex 1986: 81). An ethnic population is no more a group than a population sharing merely physical characteristics; yet either could become a group if its members developed a sense of group identity and developed the means to pursue their collective interests.

Rex is clear that the study of what is called race relations is simply a variant of the sociology of group conflict or social stratification (1986: 17). Moreover, when it comes to understanding post-war Britain he is in no doubt that 'immigrant workers relate to their society of settlement primarily through the terms of their employment and through the industrial class struggles in which they engage' (Rex 1981: 18). Not that he believes that ordinary 'colour-blind' Marxian analysis is adequate to this situation. One of his important strictures against that approach is that the relevant historical context for British race relations is not just capitalism but the social structure of the British Empire taken as a whole. Another difference with the Marxian model is the identification of class other than by reference to the mode of production or to the economy in a strict sense. He is well known for having developed the application of the concept of housing classes, where significant life-chances are determined by access to housing rather than by the division of labour or ownership of production (Rex and Moore 1967). He was thus able to demonstrate that even where non-white immigrants might be integrated in the workplace it did not mean that they were accorded the same rights as their white peers in matters of residence and education. From our point of view, what is of importance is the implication that it is natural that ethnic quasi-groups will develop forms of class action which, while in some contexts may be based on the unity of labour, in other contexts may be based upon their special situation as recipients of racial discrimination. When ethnic community organisation emerges in response to this situation it cannot be dismissed as a form of false consciousness for it is genuinely related to differential rights and status (Rex 1981: 21).

While Rex could not be accused of a view of race relations in which ethnicity is squeezed out, nevertheless the insistence that some form of class or conflict analysis is primary and all else, including ethnicity, merely serves to flesh out this form of analysis, results in a highly ambivalent view of the role of immigrant cultures and forms of life. He recognises not only racism and how it affects the behaviour of quasi-groups, but also how they will utilise their culture and sense of groupness to serve their interests; indeed he goes so far as to say:

> ... transported and migrating workers will not be simply so much dust to be blown around by capitalism either in other colonies or in the metropolis itself, but rather men, constituted by their own social and cultural systems and acting accordingly (Rex 1981: 8).

Nevertheless, he gives little indication of how ethnographic studies of ethnic quasi-groups, their internal structure and evolution, theoretically relate to his race relations paradigm. While he has no time for the grand theories of ethnicity, such as Barth's which he believes to be sociologically naive, he welcomes piecemeal studies of (quasi-) ethnic groups (Rex 1986: Chapter Five). He allows, for example, that there is 'often a considerable disparity between the way a quasi-group saw itself and the way in which others saw it', and that this is of interest to the sociologist of race relations, yet he does not offer the theoretical means of relating such discrepancies to what he sees as race relations (Rex 1986: 29). An issue such as this one — and there could be many others to do with differing perceptions on personal relationships, work, religion, and so on — cannot simply be a matter of 'fine-grain'. We do not have to accept semi-metaphysical theories of ethnicity to believe that issues about group identity, about religion and secularity, gender roles and so on have to be accommodated in a general perspective on race relations, on what kinds of conflict are likely and when, or what kind of group conscious-ness and development is likely in a given social mix, etc. Rex is clearly not against ethnographic studies and seems to believe that they are crucial to trying to understand what is likely to be the future of South Asian Muslims in Britain (Rex 1988; 1989). My point is that his paradigm of race relations as class conflict does not give any theoretical guidance on the inter-relation-ship between the modes of being of an ethnic (quasi-) group and social domination and racial inequality.[2]

Where there is an explicitly theoretical guidance on the inter-relating between the mode of being and the mode of oppression of a group, the two modes are likely to be seen as inhabiting different social worlds. An example of where this separation is theoretically embraced is Susan J. Smith. She holds that a group's racial identity is constructed by racist ideology and this identity, whether it be true or false to the group's mode of being, is the only relevant identity when the subject of study is racial inequality (Smith 1989: 12). Oppressed groups will have cultural and religious contours, but these are not relevant to the study of race relations, to the study, say, of Bangladeshis in East London. Issues of culture are of significance only when the oppressed group develops a culture of resistance to structured subordination.

Thus, the only forms of culture relevant to race relations are those which directly contribute to imposing or resisting racial inequality. Consequently, Smith argues that this allows her to dispense with the notion of 'ethnicity' (1989: 13). Ethnicity, it appears, is divided into two. Part of it may refer to aspects of resistance to racism, but the rest of it refers to culture (religion, language, national heritage, and so on), which is no less subject to historical change but is independent of colour and physical appearance and how they are used to impute race and is not, therefore, relevant to race relations.

Now it may be that this approach may prove insightful in some particular cases, in explaining perhaps the situation of some individuals who suffer discriminatory treatment from racists with whom they share a common culture. It is, however, offered as a paradigm and in that role seems very seriously limited. We are being asked to understand white attitudes, including what is referred to as common-sense or folk racism, in terms of white culture, ideology and material conditions, but without any reference to the groups of people about whom the attitudes and policies are being made. If white people say something is racial, it is racial; if they say it is not, then it is not. Similarly, if white people's view of a group's boundary changes, the group *ipso facto* changes. White attitudes may change on the basis of white perceptions about the racialised other, but there is no way of establishing that those changes are, or are not, based on fact. Racial minority groups become shadows, for by becoming all race and no ethnicity, their very existence as a group depends upon white people perceiving them. As Robert Miles, the Marxist political economist, trenchantly put it some years ago:

> The obsession of 'race relations' research with the extent and impact of racial discrimination to the exclusion of most other factors encourages a perspective in which West Indians, Pakistanis, Indians etc., come to be viewed unidimensionally as the objects of other people's beliefs and behaviour (Miles 1982: 65).

Indeed, 'race relations' becomes a misnomer for there is no group interaction, only an analysis of white racism regardless of what is happening in the internal life of the non-white groups. At best non-white groups become more like a physical, rather than a human, presence in this explanatory model, as white attitudes seem to be open to influence by everything but interaction with minority individuals and communities. It is surely necessary, when studying an inter-group relationship, to allow the possibility that new elements can be introduced from either side regardless of the limits that one side tries to impose on the nature of the relationship. Similarly, one cannot rule out in advance that what sustains or hampers a subordinate group is not radically different from what the other group(s) believe(s) to be the case.

Ethnicity and explanation

There is no shortage of examples to illustrate how both dominant and subordinate groups together contribute to outcomes. The understanding of British legislators about non-white immigrant groups was such that their attempts in the 1960s and 70s to reduce the in-flow may actually have increased the totals and certainly greatly reinforced the process of chain migration. For while those without a family bridgehead in the UK found entry impossible, groups such as the Mirpuris that were not in the first instance interested in transferring families and kinship networks to the UK increasingly found this the way to proceed (Ballard 1990). One cannot understand this process purely in terms of white fears and white structures; if Mirpuri attitudes, goals, inhibitions, kinship systems and so on were other than what they were, the outcome and the character of subsequent race relations would have been different. Or again, many people in Britain, including policy-makers, have thought of the South Asian family as oppressive and assumed ⅄ it would lead to particularly severe conflict for the generation brought up in Britain. If such predictions had proved true, the ferment within and direction of Asian communities would be other than it is; lacking the support and security of the family, Asians may well relate to each other and to the rest of society in more individualistic ways, crave greater participation in institutions beyond the community and suffer more from the rejection experienced in seeking that participation.

Would that not be race relations? Would that not be part of the subject matter for a student of race in the UK as well as for those taking stock of problems and resources and developing appropriate survival strategies? It is quite remarkable that Smith's concern, as stated on the back cover of the paperback, is with racial segregation, 'not just as a spatial form, but also as a politically constructed problem and as a socially constructed way of life' and yet ethnic minority communities, their internal structure and evolution, are ruled out in advance as irrelevant to this social process. This is despite all the evidence that shows, not only in general that there are non-white communities in Britain now with their own demands and priorities, but that specific to housing, spatial clustering cannot simply be accounted for in terms of official policies and white movements, for many minority groups are actively seeking to create localities of their own.[3] The point I am making is that it cannot be an assumption of the study of race that the dominant group can totally define a relationship, let alone that it can always predict or even control outcomes.

One can go on and say, more positively, that one cannot understand many of the aspects of ethnic minority life and socio-economic achievements, and therefore of race relations, without ethnicity. The examples I have given perhaps already illustrate this, but let me add some more. It is well known that some minorities have commercial strengths that manifest themselves at the slightest opportunity. Jews, Chinese and Indians are amongst the most notable in the context of European history and colonialism and are sometimes referred to as 'middleman minorities'. One cannot explain the role they have played without understanding colonial society, but their economic success cannot be sufficiently explained simply by that; other groups in similar situations do not perform in the same way and these groups do so not occasionally, but often. As John Stone says, this 'would suggest that certain cultural traits may be an important additional factor' (Stone 1895:98). Or again, can one really understand the differing socio-economic achievements of two Punjabi immigrant groups, the Jullunduris and Mirpuris, without a knowledge of not just the nature of their home economy and the skills they possessed but of their marriage rules and attitudes to *purdah* and clan? I think not (Ballard 1990). Again, it is interesting that the Inner London Education Authority chose to explain a report on the scholastic success of Indian children and failure of white children by reference to discipline and support at home and the nurture of ambition and role models within the family (*The Independent*, 9 March 1990). No doubt there is an element of passing the buck here, but surely one cannot dismiss the pattern of family life altogether as statistically insignificant. The editorial of the African-Caribbean newspaper *The Voice*, too, may have a point in linking differential achievement with the cultural difference between those of African and Caribbean origins (*The Voice*, 20 March 1990).

I appreciate that many people concerned with achieving racial equality in a hostile climate will be unsettled by the implications of what is being argued. Have we not reached the point of 'blaming the victim', they might ask. I appreciate that it may be precisely to foreclose the possibility of such a drift that social scientists like Susan Smith wish to dispense with the notion of ethnicity. But if so, it is a gross over-reaction. Just because ethnography can be politically abused and various studies used to justify official inaction or, worse, to reinforce racist stereotypes, does not make a whole mode of study invalid. Indeed, if we were really to take the possibility of political abuse and harmful social consequences seriously then some form of intellectual or institutional censorship would have to extend to just about all the humanities and sciences. I cannot see how there can be an intellectually valid *a priori* way of excising the possibility of blaming the victim and other forms of propaganda. The simplifications of blaming the victim have to be met by creating a more informed, sensitive and above all egalitarian climate of public debate, not by excising certain forms of study or by alternative forms of over-simplifications. For racial equality work is hardly likely to be given solid intellectual foundations where it is built on systematically excluding from analysis how a group's response to various forms of exclusion, domination and under-development is linked to its own internal modes of values and behaviour. And we certainly do not need to believe that modes of behaviour are primordial and changeless in order to see them at work — any more than one has to subscribe to a metaphysics of historical materialism in order to see the relevance of economic changes to the same analyses.

Colour, class and culture

It is, in any case, especially worth noting that while the concept of ethnicity is not without its dangers to race equality work, an ethnicity-blind approach is full of other dangers. For example, it systematically obscures the cultural dimension of racial discrimination and disadvantage. The law defines a racial group by reference to 'colour, race, nationality, or ethnic or national origins'. Though the law does not refer to class we are all aware, however, of how inferior treatment on the basis of colour can create a subordinate class which, by virtue of its socio-economic location, could continue to suffer comparative disadvantage even were colour prejudice to wane. Thus, for instance, employers who prefer a public school Oxbridge background will disadvantage the majority of society but may[4] have a disproportionately greater impact on racial minorities, and this fact is acknowledged in the legal concept of indirect discrimination. But it is less clearly recognised that this same connection with colour holds for ethnicity or culture, in the broad sense which includes community values and structure (Modood 1990a). Like class, it has no necessary relationship with colour, yet when it is linked it constitutes a dimension of race. Ethnic hierarchies and religious discrimination can and do exist in an all-white or all-black society. Nevertheless, racial groups which have distinctive or 'alien' cultural identities will suffer an additional dimension of discrimination and prejudice.[5]

Moreover, just as class can disadvantage by denying access to leisure or acquisition of skills and understanding, so can membership of a minority cultural group deprive one of, say, excellence in the dominant language and modes of thought, or access to certain forms of social networks. Again, just as colour-blind class discrimination can be a form of indirect racial discrimination, so membership of a minority community can render one less employable on the grounds of one's dress, dietary habits, or desire to take leave from work on one's holy days rather than those prescribed by the custom and practice of the majority community. Similarly, when, as in the case concerning Cleveland LEA, a local authority submits to a parental request to transfer a child from a school deemed to be insufficiently English in its cultural ambience and curriculum, the Commission for Racial Equality judges this a *prima facie* case of unlawful racial discrimination.

Colour, class and culture are then three distinct dimensions of race. Each can be the focus of prejudice and stereotyping and the other two dimensions are related to institutional discrimination. Each dimension can vary in degree (eg, the darker the skin colour the less acceptable), can be the basis of discrimination and a disadvantaged social position, though no one dimension necessarily implies another (it is possible to be black, middle-class and to be in, say, the mainstream youth culture). The worst position is where each of the dimensions is in play. The more distant an individual or group is from the norm of white middle-upper class British Christian/agnostic, the greater the marginality and exclusion. The hostility of the majority is likely to be particularly forceful if the individual in question is a member of a community (and not just a free-floating or assimilated individual) which is sufficiently numerous to reproduce itself as a community and has a distinctive and cohesive value system which can be perceived as an alternative and possible challenge to the norm. The Rastifarians are one example of where these three dimensions are active; Bradford's Muslim devotionalists are another.

Anti-racism and identity

The Satanic Verses affair is not a one-off. A close reading of newspapers will reveal that as many race relations battles turn on issues of culture and minority rights as on colour discrimination and socio-economic deprivation. Anti-racists seem to be slow to recognise that it is ethnic communities, no less than colour and class, that lie at the heart of race and race relations today. The root of this inability lies in creating race exclusively from the point of view of the dominant whites and failing to recognise that those whom white people treat as no more than the raw material of racist categorisation have indeed a mode of being of their own which defies reduction to racist categorisation. We need a concept of race that helps us to understand that any oppressed group feels its oppression most according to those dimensions of its being which it (not the oppressor) values the most; moreover, it will resist its oppression from those dimensions of its being from which it derives its greatest collective psychological strength. Let me illustrate the point by reference to Muslims once again. They hardly ever think of themselves in terms of colour or in terms of race as defined by, say, Smith. And so, in terms of their own being they feel most acutely those problems that the anti-racists are blind to; and respond weakly to those challenges that the anti-racists want to meet with most force. For this reason, and because of their own racism, Muslims cannot easily, confidently or systematically assume the moral high ground on the issue of colour-racism; their sense of being and their surest conviction about their devaluation by others comes from their historical community of faith and from their critique of 'the West'.

Authentic anti-racism for Muslims, therefore, will inevitably have a religious dimension and take a form in which it is integrated with the rest of Muslim concerns. Anti-racism begins (i.e. ought to begin) by accepting oppressed groups on their own terms (knowing full well that these will change and evolve), not by imposing a spurious identity and asking them to fight in the name of that. The new strength amongst Muslims youths in, for example, not tolerating racial harassment owes no less to Islamic re-assertion than to metropolitan anti-racism: people do not turn and run when something they care about is under attack. The racist taunt 'Rushide' rouses more self-defence than 'black bastard'. Too many anti-racists see the racism but are happy to be ignorant of the living identities that racism obscures: South Asians who experience racial discrimination are reduced to discriminated beings ('blacks') who happen to be Asians (Modood 1988).

Muslims are wiser here than radical anti-racists: in locating oneself in a hostile society one must begin with one's mode of being, not one's mode of oppression, for one's strength flows from one's mode of being. British thinking on race, following the American lead, has regarded the descendants of African slaves in the New World as the paradigm of a racial group. The historical oppression of this group, however, has been such that its mode of being has become virtually identical to its mode of oppression, that is to say, the materialist's claim that they are what white society has made them achieves some surface plausibility. Though even here it is notable that one of the significant strands in the movement by black Americans to achieve dignity and self-respect has been what is understood as at least a partial rediscovery of an ancestral Islam.

The disowning of slave names is a simple but effective illustration of the point I am making: Cassius Clay is the name of the mode of oppression, Muhammad Ali is the name of the mode of being. If dogmatic anti-racists continue to define racism and anti-racism in terms of the primacy of the mode of oppression, they will shut out Asians and other minorities, fail to understand them and cut them off from the sources of their group pride. And group pride is the motor without which racial equality is impossible.

55

Legal concept of race

I believe that we in Britain are slowly learning that our concepts of racial equality need to be tuned not just to guaranteeing that individuals of different hues are treated alike but also to the fact that Britain now encompasses communities with different norms, cultures and religions. Hence racial equality cannot always mean that our public institutions and the law itself must treat everybody by the norms and convenience of the majority. Local authorities have been discovering this, especially with regard to schools, where some attempts have been made, usually in the glare of adverse publicity, to make provision for minority religions and languages, celebrate non-Christian religious festivals and even to adjust school holidays to coincide with some of them. More interesting and less publicised are the ways that the law has begun to take cognisance of the new cultural plurality (Poulter 1986, 1989, 1990). Occasionally this has been at the level of statute such as with the 1976 exemption of turban-wearing Sikhs from the legal requirement to wear a crash helmet when riding a motor-bike, a principle which has recently been extended to exempt Sikhs from the new compulsory rule that persons on construction sites must wear safety helmets (Employment Act 1989, ss. 11 and 12); there is also the indirect provision for Sikhs to continue to be able to wear their kirpans (religious daggers) in public places without being guilty of an offence (Criminal Justice Act 1988, s. 139 (5) (b)). More often it is the judiciary that acknowledges the relevance of cultural difference to racial equality and, therefore, to race (Banton 1988, 1989). Sometimes this is in the application of the Race Relations Act (1976) such as the House of Lords judgement that allows Sikh males to wear turbans in schools (and, by extension, places of work) regardless of the rules of the school (or employer) (Mandla v Dowell Lee, 1983); or the Industrial Tribunal decisions which have allowed that in appropriate circumstances Asian women may wear trousers at work but not other women (Malik v British Home Stores, 1980); or that a Rastifarian cannot be refused employment merely because he is unwilling to cut off his dreadlocks (Dawkins v Crown Supplies 1989).[6]

In each of these cases an important aspect of a person's religious or cultural practice was protected by law and made a difference to his or her treatment by the courts. Such a principle can be sharply contrasted with the famous case in France in 1989 which revealed the lack of a right of Muslim girls to wear the *hijab* in a state school in France; when a similar conflict arose in a Cheshire school in January 1990 the school was soon forced to back down by public opinion as well as by the force of legal precedent. Yet it is important to note that this religious and cultural protection in Britain is far from comprehensive (the parochialism of the law of blasphemy is a case in point) and more importantly that it is indirectly derived from race legislation. It is not, for example, the right of Muslim women to wear modest dress at work but the right only of women from those ethnic groups in Britain in which Muslims are a significant number (Modood, 1992b). White Muslim women, for instance, have no rights in this regard, as some new young converts have discovered (*Today* 1990) and so the law would have a better grip on the social reality of racial discrimination if it were broadened to make direct discrimination against Muslims unlawful in the same way that it currently protects the employment and other rights of religious minorities such as Sikhs and Jews.[7] The cultural sensitivity of the courts does however go beyond merely deciding on cases of racial discrimination. In two cases, for example, the English courts have been prepared to enforce contracts for the payment of deferred dowry (mahr) by Muslim husbands upon divorce (*Shahnaz v Rizwan* 1965; *Qureshi v Qureshi* 1972) and in May 1990 a High Court Judge awarded a divorced Asian women £20,000 damages against her husband, who had slandered her by suggesting she was not a virgin at the time of her marriage, on the grounds that the insult was very grave in her community (*Seemi v Sadiq*).

Equality Through Pluralism

Each of these examples of statute and judgement is small but, taken together, they offer an intimation of a policy approach that might be called equality through pluralism. What I have in mind is not new, not peculiar to Muslims, nor special to Britain. Indeed, integration through pluralism rather than assimilation — what has been called 'the ethnicity paradox' — was observed and advocated in the first quarter of this century by the American sociologists, E Parks and W I Thomas, in respect of the European and Southern black immigration to cities such as Chicago.[8] The 'ethnicity paradox' refers to their conviction that allowing ethnic communities to take root and flourish in the new soil was the most satisfactory way of promoting long term integration and participation in the institutions of the wider American community. They argued that not only did immigrant institutions meet the special cultural needs of a community, but they provided a basis for continuity for people who were particularly caught in severe and destabilising change. Even more importantly, they were a source of an individual's self-esteem and status, which otherwise suffered from the devaluation that the immigrant experienced; moreover, they enabled a group pride and could lead to a rise in status and respect for the group as a whole and, therefore, stem the need to disown one's origins in order to succeed in the new society. They also recognised that ethnic group organisations bring control to areas of urban life that may lack it and, most importantly, give immigrant groups some control over their own adaptation to the new society. This allows them to adapt in an atmosphere of relative security as opposed to one of rootlessness and powerlessness, where each individual is forced to come to terms with a new society in relative isolation and, therefore, exclusively on the terms of the majority. Park and Thomas noted that immigrants:

> ... who began by deserting their group end by attempting to improve the status of these groups ... seeking to make something with which a man may be proud to identify himself. The fact that the individual will

not be respected unless the group is respected becomes thus perhaps the most sincere source of nationalist movements in America. To this extent the nationalist movements represent an effort to increase participation in American life (Park and Miller, 1921: 143-144).

This, then, is what has been called the ethnicity paradox — allowing more space to ethnic minority communities to do their own thing enables them to become a feature of the new society and creates a secure base from which participation in the institutions of the wider society follows. It is interesting that similar arguments surfaced amongst American black activists and young intellectuals in the later 1960s and 1970s when, after decades in which race egalitarians strenuously denied that there was any such thing as black culture, fearing that an acknowledgement of difference was the thin end of the wedge of inequality, blacks began to celebrate their African roots and what arose from them in the American soil. Perhaps the symbolic high-point to date of this movement was the recent public rejection by Jesse Jackson, not without echoes in this country (Dennis 1989; Yekawi 1986: 103), of the highly politicised term 'black' in favour of 'African-American' as a public identity. Materialist theories of anti-racism typically underestimate these feelings and the positive role of ethnic pride. The 'black is beautiful' campaign reached far more American blacks than the civil rights campaign and indeed provided a personal and collective psychological dynamic which fed into the former and which enabled blacks to take advantage of the socio-economic opportunities created by the politics.

Despite the ethnic assertiveness that is visible in many places, and of which the Asian Muslims are simply the most prominent current example, our race theorising lags behind that of Jesse Jackson. Indeed, it has been suggested that arguments such as these will only lead to 'a further marginalisation of 'Asians' in general and Muslims in particular' for it is said that they, unlike blacks, will not so readily win acceptance in the cultural mainstream (Gilroy 1989). I think this judgement usefully alerts us to a danger, but is based on too restricted a view. The creation of social integration and racial equality has to run with the grain of ethnicity, not against it. In the 1980s we learnt that these goals could not be achieved by being 'colour-blind'. The lesson of the 1990s will, I believe, be that these goals cannot be achieved by being 'ethnic-blind'. For everybody is a somebody, not just a victim. A mature anti-racism rests on the appreciation of the dialectical relationship between what a racial group thinks it is and how others treat it. For, by definition, to be a racial group is to be suspended between these two modalities of existence; British race sociology and the anti-racism it informs has too long looked at the world with one eye shut.

Notes

1. The same kind of group pride and self-definition that is evidenced in other movements. Cf. the founding statement of the New York Gay Liberation Front: 'We are stepping out of these roles and simplistic myths. WE ARE GOING TO BE WHO WE ARE'.

2. John Rex's thinking has been developed and modified in the light of theoretical challenges and socio-political situations and continues to be so. In commenting on an earlier draft of this article, he has written to me that he now believes that not only can a class analysis not fully account for some of the current 'racial' conflicts in British society, but that he believes that the notion of class interest has to be supplemented with the Weberian notion of religious interest, at least in respect of Muslim communities.

3. It is interesting that what is now a commonplace truth was, when originally stated by Badr Dahya (1974) in reference to Rex's thesis about Pakistanis and housing in Birmingham, regard with unease. Perhaps there is a lesson here for those anxious about admitting the fact of ethnicity into race relations work.

4. I say 'may' because there is now evidence that some non-white groups have university places, including at Oxbridge, in excess of their proportion of the population. Thus, for example, British Chinese form about 0.25% of 18-24 year olds, and British Indians about 1.75%, but formed 1.1% and 2.6% respectively of the students admitted to Cambridge University in 1991 (Modood, forthcoming).

5. Thus nobody is confused when a vicar who describes Islam as an 'alien *culture* thriving in our midst' is admonished by the Bishop of Wakefield as having 'set back *race* relations 20 years' and the story is reported in a popular newspaper under the headline: Vicar's 'alien *race*' jibe makes a Bishop see red' (my italics throughout), *Daily Express*, 9 March 1990.

6. The decision recognising Rastafarians as an ethnic group was overturned by a majority of 2-1 at the Employment Appeals Tribunal, *Crown Suppliers* (PSA) v. *Dawkins* April 24, 1991.

7. In *Nyazi v. Rymans Ltd* (10.5.88 EAT 6(38), the Employment Appeals Tribunal upheld an industrial tribunal's ruling that Muslims are not a 'racial group' for the purposes of a complaint under the Race Relations Act 1976. The recent IT decision in *CRE v. Precision* (26.7.91) confirms that a refusal to employ someone because he or she is a Muslim is not unlawful direct discrimination though in many circumstances it would be unlawful discrimination. Cases such as these have led the CRE to consider whether legislation is now needed to cover explicitly religious discrimination and incitement to religious hatred, Commision for Racial Equality, *Second Review of the Race Relations Act 1976*, (London, June 1991).

8. The term 'ethnicity paradox' is Barbara Lal's and I am indebted to her for my understanding of Park and Thomas. See Lal 1983, reworked as Lal 1990: Chapter Five.

Source: *New Community*, vol 17(1) October 1990.

8

New Maps for old: emergent ethnicities

Review of How Many Miles to Bablyon? Adewale Maja-Pearce, Heinemann

This essay, by a man who is Scottish-Nigerian not only by parentage but also by upbringing, is about belonging, about the difficulties (and some advantages) posed by having more than one heritage, and about not being white in Britain. There is a critique of Little Englander racism, but there are also some hard words about West Africa, as well as black and Asian immigrants and their champions. The essay is a celebration not only of the longing to be rooted, but of the sense of physically belonging in a familiar landscape.

People who are securely rooted, especially if privileged, envy outsiders. Those who are outsiders, usually without any choice in the condition, envy the rooted. The book, based in Britain, continues a search for personal identity that an earlier book revealed was not to be found in Nigeria. For, as many Asians have also found, nothing is guaranteed to reveal one's Britishness as much as travel in the land of one's fathers. The problem is not in the discovery, but in making the British accept it. Here, perhaps, is the real significance of writers such as Maja-Pearce, and others, such as Kwesi Owusu and Ferdi Dennis, who are trying to place themselves in contemporary Britain. What is sought is a hyphenated cultural identity, in which Anglicised sensibilities are enlivened and broadened with a genuine interest in West Africa.

Maja-Pearce has an unromantic view of marginality and the sub-cultures beloved of sociologists. Much of the essay revolves around his one-time involvement with social flotsam and jetsam. This distorts the balance of the book, for the main immigrant experience is not of free-floating outsiders, but of tight networks and strong family obligations. The central issue is not the pain of not belonging, but of how and when to let go of communal ties. This comes out, but rather late in the essay, when he focuses on Asian experience. However, his distance from the people he speaks of leads him to see them

61

only in terms of problems. He is thus able to see that specially 'obsessive hatred of people from the Indian sub-continent', but has nothing positive to report about the people concerned. This is not an unimportant omission in someone who berates Ray Honeyford for doing the same thing.

The questions Maja-Pearce raises about race and ethnicity are important, even if his answers are not satisfactory. He sees that the emphasis on colour-racism is too narrow as a basis for understanding race relations in Britain. But he falls into the opposite danger of failing to recognise how colour is thoroughly mixed up in the identity issues he discusses, and that colour-racism has a weight of its own, regardless of other burdens. He is right that, for some, colour-racism is an excuse for all their ills. But the important truth is that those who analyse race relations in terms of racism, and those who analyse it in terms of 'culture-clash', are offering a false choice. His own essay can be cited as witness to this. He seems to believe that the reality of racism and race relations lies in cultural tensions that are falsely characterised in terms of colour. Yet his analysis of racists uncovers a cultural chauvinism by which entire peoples, identified on the basis of colour, are written off as worthless because of their alleged lack of, or inferior, culture.

This is surely one of the most prominent forms of racism in Britain, and may be characterised as cultural racism. Groups are opposed, feared, despised and stereotyped, in terms of *both* their colour and their culture. This combination makes their oppression more acute, even though some individuals can escape on one or the other front. It follows that remedies must address both dimensions of this duality: just attacking colour prejudice will not remove the hostility that has built up against some non-white groups.

The problem is formidable, but we are not wholly without resources. The law, for instance, uses a more complex notion of discrimination than Maja-Pearce. He thinks of it as a deliberate, conscious act of prejudice, and so does not see how British society creates more and higher hurdles for non-white people. These hurdles may often be made of class and culture, but can still constitute indirect racial discrimination.

Source: *The Times*, 20 October 1990

Review of **Black British, White British: A History of Race Relations in Britain**, Dilip Hiro, Grafton Books

How many 20 year old books on race relations can be updated simply by adding extra chapters? Most would need to be radically recast in order to harmonise the older text with the new. It is an achievement of Dilip Hiro's book, first published in 1971 and revised in 1973, that it has stood the test of two decades so well that the new chapters, such as the one on the Rushdie affair, cohere with the earlier material. Indeed, the concluding chapter, which predicts that racism and unassimilating minorities will be a long-term feature of the British social landscape, is left virtually unaltered.

The book's three equal parts look at the subject from the respective points of view of West Indians, Asians and white Britons. Its strength lies in its historico-cultural perspective. Put rather simply, the thesis is that, while the determining feature of the African-Caribbean psyche and community life is the historical experience of racial slavery, for Asians it is the threat to their traditional forms of collectivism; and for whites, the attitudes of superiority sustained by a centuries-old relationship of dominance-subservience. While Hiro does not exclude the relevance of other perspectives, it is notable that in the new chapters there is much more on socio-cultural issues than on, say, jobs and the economy.

In 1973, he was sufficiently persuaded by the sociologists to write that whites withheld social acceptance from West Indian and Asian immigrants primarily because they are racially different from the white British. He now writes that, in the case of Asians, prejudice stems as much from consider-ations of culture as of colour. This theme is heard increasingly as Asians begin to articulate the racism they encounter and attack the perception of 'Oriental' cultures as inferior, backward and barbaric. For Asians face a dual oppression, of colour and of culture. While the 1980s anti-racists believed that organising around colour was the most effective form of resistance, it is now obvious that any strategy that does not tap into the resources of cultural pride will not draw Asians into it.

We would all have gained if the race thinking of the past two decades had included this historico-cultural approach, rather than consisting of a duopoly of urban-conflict sociology and variations of Marxism. Perhaps this duopoly was beyond intellectual challenge until social developments produced their own refutation. The key here is the emergence of Asian communities (as opposed to an Asian presence in the labour force) at the centre of British race relations. Before this, the Asian experience remained mutely encapsulated by a sociology that drew its inspiration from Notting Hill or Detroit or Soweto — anywhere but from South Asian societies.

Of course, we need above all to understand what happened to these societies under British imperialism, but no one will achieve that unless they have made an effort to comprehend them in the first place. To suppose that we can understand the oppressed solely by a critique of the mechanisms of oppression is not only intellectually flawed. As we will increasingly see, as cultural pride and ethnic identity come to the fore as sites of struggle, it does not produce equality in the context of social pluralism.

Twenty years ago, Hiro caused some consternation when he argued that 'integration' was an impossible ideal, yet his view is now commonplace. It will be interesting to see if he is equally prescient in his observation that the logic of events is leading to the incorporation of Muslim family law into the British legal system.

Source: *New Stateman and Society*, May 1991

Review of **Ethnicity and Nationalism in Post-Imperial Britain**, Harry Goulbourne, Cambridge University Press

When even those who a decade or so ago were arguing that non-white ethnicities were melting into the pot of Black politics, and that ethnicity was a construct of the New Right bent on perceiving cultural differences where there were none, now speak of ethnicity; when young Jews, after several generations of Anglicisation, are asserting their difference from rather than their similarity to the rest of the population; when the Irish are lobbying for inclusion in race equality monitoring forms; it is hard to quarrel with Harry Goulbourne that ethnicity is stimulating a redefinition of what it means to be British today. He fears that the celebration of difference and the assertion of group interests has gone too far and is playing into the hands of those who would define British nationality as white ethnicity. For if everyone is being encouraged to think of themselves in terms of ethnic membership, then the majority too will think of themselves in this way and wish to exercise their right to have their country, their homeland, reflect their historical traditions and norms. This will legitimise the view of ethnic minorities as aliens, in Britain but not fully of Britain, will jeopardise the commitment to racial equality and will thereby lead to endemic social conflict and the breakdown of give-and-take democratic politics. It is perhaps an indication of the urgency of these issues that this pessimistic view of multi-culturalism, heard for a number of years from writers such as Ray Honeyford, should now be put forward by a British West Indian scholar in race relations.

Goulbourne wants, however, to disconnect the pessimistic view from an association with ethnic majoritarian or white nationalism. Indeed, his argument is that the new nationalism derived from Enoch Powell and debated in the pages of *The Salisbury Review* is in the same intellectual stable as multi-culturalism, for both use the language of group rights and are concerned with the preservation of stale cultural identities by political means. His own appeal is to what he calls traditional nationalism which is based on territory, in which groups based on race, language, or religion have no rights, but in which all individuals have the same rights, and are able to belong freely to one or more or no cultural groups; none is excluded from the definition of the nation on the basis of their group membership but no group allows group loyalties to compromise national loyalty. The distinction between traditional and ethnic nationalism, however, is over-stated, for the case of groups like the Croatians and the Ukranians does not depend upon an appeal to a new kind of nationalism and would be readily familiar to nineteenth century European nationalists. In any case, even if in certain parts of the world we are witnessing excessive and dangerous petty nationalisms, Goulbourne shows more panic than judgement in suggesting that Britain is at the forefront of these developments.

Where Goulbourne does make an important point is in emphasising that no society can survive unless most people are willing to recognise and develop what they have in common. Here the silence of the multiculturalists can be politically divisive, but Goulbourne's way of making this point is itself politically unhelpful. *The Swann Report,* the bible of British multi-culturalism, is clear, as Goulbourne recognises, that we need commonality *and* diversity and that this does mean engaging with the concept of Britishness. Goulbourne may be right to point out that no adequate theoretical statement of this view has yet appeared and that many multiculturalists tend to speak of diversity only, but he is wrong to conclude that we must therefore choose between a sense of nationhood and distinctive ethnic identities. A better way would be to emphasize that talk of diversity does not make logical or practical sense outside a secure framework of commonality.

A deeper problem with his distinction between nation-states that create a common nationality out of a territorial unit of rule and states created as homelands for an ethnic group is to overlook that the viability of the former, for example Britain or France, depended upon questions of religion, language and ethnicity being settled by a compromise or by the presence of a dominant group able to impose its terms upon others. The contemporary ethnic assertiveness in such traditional nation-states is not so much about ethnic purity and separatism but about the historical and new minority groups demanding a re-negotiation of the previous terms. Again, this is not because of a failure of liberal politics in favour of a new groupism, but is the development of liberal democratic concern with minorities. Politics and law depend upon some degree of cultural and value commonality and inevitably reflect the norms and values of the society that they are part of. In this sense, no state stands outside culture or ethnicity and changes in these will need to be reflected in the arrangements of the state.

A complementary line of argument that Goulbourne has against multiculturalism (or as he calls it, 'the new pluralism') is that it replaces the politics of racial justice with a concern for preservation of minority cultures. Yet this too is an untenable distinction for, as the Swann Committee found, ensuring parity of esteem for disadvantaged groups who are defined by culture as well as colour cannot be achieved without developing a concept of cultural-racism. The ways in which minorities are stereotyped, marginalised and allowed to succeed only where they pay the price of disowning their origins is much more to do with rejection on the basis of (mis)perceived culture rather than biology. This means that racial equality cannot be achieved where minority cultures are held to be illegitimate in Britain. Egalitarians, not for the first time, find themselves paradoxically having to draw attention to what they ultimately hope becomes taken for granted: just as colour-racism cannot be over-turned by closing one's eyes to existing attitudes to colour difference, so cultural-racism cannot even be identified by denying the fact or legitimacy of cultural differences.

While Goulbourne's central arguments then do not establish a conclusive case against the politics of ethnicity, there are nevertheless interesting insights on the way. He is shrewdly aware of the competition between different minority groups to win sympathy for their sectional causes and of the need to avoid comparisons between different groups at the expense of each other. He does not, however, always follow his own advice for, while sensitive to the possible stereotyping involved in the view that West Indians are confrontational, he himself uses throwaway remarks about 'strident demands by militant Muslims' and dismisses religious anger as 'fanaticism and irrationality'. There are also two case studies of diasporic politics, those of Sikhs and Guyanese, looking at how homeland politics can divert groups from becoming part of Britain in spirit as well as in fact. He argues that this happens much less with those from the Caribbean than South Asia, for while the former is a region of order and democracy, instability and conflict in the latter region continue to be a cause of concern for the Asia diaspora. This is linked to the interesting view that a tradition of non-militant nationalism in the former British Caribbean inclines West Indians here to liberal individualism and to eschew the politicisation of ethnicity.

Yet this is to ignore the African-Caribbean lead in the politics of colour-conciousness, whether it be in the form of black power romanticism of the sort which applauded Malcolm X's concept of 'white devils' before his embrace of the humanism of Islam, or Rastafarianism in the 1970s, or the Black Sections and GLC-style forms of anti-racism in the 1980s. Goulbourne stands for a genuine strand in moderate West Indian thinking which needs to be heard; but there is no point pretending that this strand is the principal contribution of black activism to British politics. He is right when he says that West Indian agitation created a bridgehead of racial equality which other minorities have taken advantage of; but this also applies to the pluralism he deplores. The beginning of the politics of *difference* is the claim that no one who has not suffered as Blacks have suffered can understand it and hence only Black people can lead the struggle, have a right to organise autonomously, have separate representation etc. His failure to appreciate this is linked to his strategy of attacking soft rather than hard left targets and ignoring the contribution of the New Left, and especially of radical feminism, to the erosion of the universalistic conceptions of justice and citizenship to which he appeals.

Groups that used to be 'coloured' became for some years 'black' and are now becoming 'non-white'. This is perhaps the first book to use comprehensively the new term though without offering any reasons to do so except noting in passing that 'black' belongs to the field of political choice and not analysis. This in fact ignores how in the 1980s it had become a term of political imposition and that the search for a new terminology marks the failure of the Left to appropriate the new ethnic identities for its own use.

Source: *The Times Literary Supplement,* 24 January 1992

Muslim
assertiveness

9

The Rushdie Affair: texts and contexts

One cannot but be struck by the tone of Salman Rushdie's *In Good Faith*. Its willingness to discuss the issue with Muslims, let alone its self-discipline and cool temper, is in contrast to Mr Rushdie's last published statement (*Observer,* 22 January 1989, three weeks before the murderous *fatwa*), in which angry Muslims were dismissed as agents of the forces of darkness. It also contrasts with his refusal to treat his Muslim critics with any seriousness in the three months when their anger was not a news item. If this essay had come 12 months earlier, who knows what the Ayatollah would have done, certainly the climate of debate in Britain would have been very different.

For me there are many things of value in *The Satanic Verses.* While not in the same league of enjoyment as *Midnight's Children,* it is nevertheless delightful to read Urdu colloquialisms and Bombay bazaar talk woven so effortlessly and wittily into the fabric of English. I cannot pretend to follow the book at all points, but follow enough to see myself and my family — our treasures and sorrows and evolution — in the mirror of its imagination. Rushdie's celebration of our migration and metamorphosis is, despite its inaccessibility to the non-literary, of deep significance to British Asian Muslims.

Islam has more than one aspect. It has been the ethical inspiration that has given its adherents the power not just of physical conquest but also a dynamic in which other civilisations are delved for understanding. The Arabic word for knowledge, *ilm,* is second only to *Allah* in its frequency in the Qur'an. The prophet Muhammad himself urged the need to learn from all cultures: 'Seek knowledge, even unto China'. Moreover, the Qur'an is explicit that its message is not be set apart from other religions. It is in direct continuity with all previous revelations and encompasses all that is true in other faiths. This gave the early Muslims not only confidence in themselves but also the confidence to seek synthesis with other cultures. The flow of traffic has not been one way. Muslims are proud that they provided the historical foundations of the Renaissance of Europe — something that Europeans, however, have systematically erased from their consciousness because of the pain to their self-image.

Mr Rushdie's celebration of our hybridity (it makes no more sense to be ashamed of oneself because one cannot be like one's parents than to be ashamed of them because they are not like the white people on television) is of significance because there is a danger of Islam in Britain becoming a religion of the ghetto, an ethnic totem in a facile 'multi-culturalism'. The current temper of British Asian Muslims, partly as a consequence of the injuring and harassing power of *The Satanic Verses,* is not to seek the common ground, but to emphasise difference. Two centuries of European domination and racism have badly bruised the self- confidence of Muslims. What happens at this stage could prevent us from moving on from wounded assertiveness to a dialogue among equals.

It is an understatement to say that *The Satanic Verses* has made the development of a confident, outward-looking British Islam rather less than more likely. Still, one has to live with that. What one should not have to live with, and it is clear that Muslims cannot, is the passages which reduce Islam to a sexual appetite: the vulgar language, the sexual imagery, the attribution of lustful motives, without evidence, to the Prophet. In his essay, Rushdie says this, like the rest of the book, is offered in the spirit of radical dissent and criticism. Apparently, it is supposed to assist Muslims (and those of other faiths) to reconsider the relationship between religion, sex and the role of women. These are important questions but where is the argument that shows that these questions can only be raised in these cheap and offensive ways? Where is the argument that Muslims will best be helped to approach such profound topics in these perverse ways?

It is here that Rushdie wants to exercise his right to freedom of expression, including ways of expression that give offence, should he prefer to use them. But why should society give the artist *this* right? Why should Muslims not spit back the criticism because they do not like the way it is (out of a preference) spat at them? It is this, not the criticism but its manner, which has hurt, angered and shamed Muslims and made the sound of Rushdie's name vile to their ears. It is not the political ambitions of fundamentalism (virtually non-existent in Britain) but the lashings as felt by simple, perhaps too simple, devotionalism that has prevented Muslims from thinking about virtually anything else for a year.

It may be that the rest if the population has become used to living with such modes of criticism of what they hold most sacred. But different cultural groups will value such literature in different degrees depending on their history and the vulnerabilities of their position. While some groups may be able positively to use irreverence, others may be demoralised and disabled by it.

Inhibitions of this sort, unlike the principle of absolute freedom of expression, are entirely consistent with English liberalism which has since the time of T. H. Green been committed to balancing the rights of individuals with the good of the community. For it is only in the context of shared conventions and responsibilities that rights arise and can be met. The artist without social responsibility who provokes anger where there can be no dialogue threatens the field of discourse itself. Twentieth-century liberal politics has successfully resisted the individualism of Herbert Spencer and John Stuart Mill, of Max Stirner and Nietzsche and recognised that where internalised restraints break down, social harmony and other goals must be protected by means of law. We should not succumb to the libertarianism which sees the artist as a Nietzchean *übermensch,* towering above conventional morality with perfect liberty to publish imaginative exploration regardless of social consequences. In most cases the necessary inhibitions will be acquired through habit, sympathy and public censure. But where they are lacking and civility is threatened, the law may be the only recourse.

The tone of Rushdie's essay is unreservedly to be welcomed. It is a tone which is absent from *The Satanic Verses,* absent from Mr Rushdie's dismissal of Muslims' petitions and incompatible with the demand to bring out the paperback. That incompatibility will nullify the good that Mr Rushdie seeks to do with the essay.

Source: *The Independent,* 5 February 1990.

Review of A Satanic Affair: Salman Rushdie and the rage of Islam, Malise Ruthven, Chatto and Windus

If blazing red covers and sensational titles reflected contents this would be an unbearable book. Indeed, Malise Ruthven's analysis of Muslim protests, arguments and leaders is unsympathetically partisan, sometimes sheer tabloid (can he really think that the powerless Bradford Muslims are 'a kind of Raj in reverse'?). He sees the self-righteous sense of moral superiority of Muslims but not that of the libertarians, which is no less in evidence today.

Nevertheless, it is worth bearing with Ruthven. He writes with understanding and acuity about the socio-cultural dimensions of South Asian Islam, the veneration of the Prophet (deemed by many Muslims to be excessive), of notions of communal honour and anxiety about absorption into a hegemonic culture that so many Muslims, not least working-class, believe is a threat to their identity and decency.

Ruthven draws attention to all the evidence that shows that the Muslim anger in India and in England was spontaneous, not engineered. He points to the pre-publication interviews that Rushdie gave in India where he announced frankly that *The Satanic Verses* would cause Muslims soul-searching offence — western audiences, however, were being told that the book was about 'migration, metamorphosis, divided selves, love, death' — and concludes that thereafter, amid all the hype generated by Penguin to recoup a £850,000 advance, it was impossible for Muslims not to notice the book. Yet in other passages he sees fundamentalist puppeteers at work. While this is overplayed, Ruthven does a useful task in revealing not just the Iranian but the extent of the unhelpful Saudi involvement in British Muslim affairs.

Ruthven is alive to the Asian-ness of the issue. For leaving aside Teheran (which in any case came late on to the scene), the demonstrations, whether in Johannesberg or Bradford, Bombay or Islamabad, have all been by South Asians. Not only have there been no major demonstrations in other Muslim countries but the only country in Western Europe or North America to have seen ongoing protest is Britain. This cannot be because of the size of Britain's Muslim population, for there are more Muslims in France, Germany and USA. Rather, Britain is the only western country to have a significant Asian Muslim working class. And while fundamentalism is primarily a movement of the educated middle class, the devotionalism of the Prophet is strongest among the rural peasantry from which Pakistani and Bangladeshi immigrants to Britain, unlike those to USA, originate (see Modood 1990b on diverse nature of Asian Muslims).

Accordingly, Ruthven is one of the few to see parallels with the Ray Honeyford affair in which, too, there was a clash between community honour and freedom of speech. The issues of multi-culturalism which were crudely suppressed then are again on the agenda with the significant difference that in the Honeyford case, the left took the stand that freedom of speech did not mean a licence to insult minority communities. With certain honourable exceptions, the left seems no longer to wish to uphold that principle.

While Ruthven questions some of Rushdie's coarse language and his insensitive provocation, he is in no doubt that *The Satanic Verses* is a serious work of art. He is wholly opposed to any form of blasphemy law but argues that the Race Relations Act needs to be extended to include sectarian insults. He doesn't, however, believe that Rushdie's book would fall foul of such a law, for he thinks that it is saved by the serious artistic *intention* of the author. This is a surprising conclusion, for the Race Relations Act and the incitement to hatred clauses are as much concerned with social consequences as with the intentions of individuals.

What is at issue in this controversy is not blasphemy, if by this is meant a falsehood against God. *The Satanic Verses* ignited Muslims because it was felt as an outrage against all those whose own honour depends upon upholding the honour of the revered. Ruthven gets close to the truth here but does not quite grasp it. He explains the Muslim anger in terms of *izzat* or honour. Of course *izzat* is important to Muslims but the issue here is *ghairat*: while the former is about the respect others accord to one, the latter is about the quality of one's pride or love. While *izzat* is something to be maintained *ghairat* is something to be tested. (A case of national *ghairat* was the British response to the invasion of the Falklands.) *The Satanic Verses* is for some Muslims a challenge to demonstrate their attachment to and love for their faith: their *imani ghairat*. It does not follow from this of course that *ghairat* requires a violent response; on the contrary, the Prophet himself practised tolerance and forgiveness.

What prospective legislation or institutional remedy (a Writers' Code on minorities administered by the equivalent of the Press Council?) can prevent such conflict needs to be seriously debated, for without it it is doubtful whether British Muslims can be drawn out of their present alienation from the society that is now their home.[1]

If Rushdie had successfully attacked fundamentalism as I believe he intended, many Muslims would have cheered and certainly there would not be the present lines of confrontation. It was not the exploration of religious doubt but the lampooning of the Prophet that provoked the anger. This sensitivity has nothing to do with Quranic fundamentalism. It is to do with South Asian reverence of Muhammad, and cultural insecurity as experienced in the UK and even more profoundly in India. Khomeni's uninvited intervention was purely political[2]. A *fatwa* is a learned legal opinion; it is not a trial, not a verdict, not a sentence. By turning it into a sentence Khomeni placed himself outside Islamic law, and though by so doing he spoke to the hearts of many Muslims who felt despised, powerless and without recourse in law, he nevertheless in one stroke jeopardised community relations in Britain.

Those who are using this affair to talk up confrontation between Islam and the West are being grossly irresponsible, as are those who are demanding a paperback without even a preface to appease the British Muslim community. We desperately need a negotiated settlement to this crisis (the present death toll is 30); editorial writers should not encourage Rushdie to climb the ladder of escalation. If he cares for British Muslims or for Britain he should make his peace with us regardless of what they say or do in Teheran.

References

1. My direct contribution to this debate is Modood 1990c.
2. I have come to revise this judgement. The Ayatollah's *fatwa* of 14 February 1989 was an immediate (indeed, too immediate) and direct response to the death of ten demonstrators in Islambad, Pakistan on 12 February and the five deaths in Srinigar, India on the 13th. It is uncharitable to suppose that the motives or intended significance could have been purely political.

Source: *The Times Higher Education Supplement*, 30 March 1990

A Review of **A Brief History of Blasphemy**, Richard Webster, The Orwell Press

The Rushdie affair raises so many large issues — artistic freedom and responsibility, ideas of the sacred, secularism, minority rights, racism and cultural hegemony — that, however the immediate politics of it may turn, it will generate ideas and emotions for decades. Yet one might suppose that, having engaged the minds and hearts of so many for 18 months, the main lines of development have already been publicly aired. Richard Webster's penetrating book is proof that this is not the case. Most people will find new insights in it and some liberals, in particular, might be forced to rethink their stand.

Webster states his position at the outset. He believes that Salman Rushdie is suffering a cruel injustice in the form of the *fatwa*, and that we must protect him; but he also suggests that we must help him to go beyond what might be called the Mike Gatting theory of responsibility: if people get killed or hurt demonstrating against me it is nothing to do with me.

Most writing on this affair has revolved around the question: what is it about Muslims that makes them respond in the way they have done? Webster asks what it is about contemporary Western culture that allows literary obscenities to be hurled, even in good faith, against Muslims. His answer, like those which connect *racial* anti-semitism to centuries of *religious* anti-semitism, is that contemporary Muslim bashing is, often unknown to itself, a rehearsal of hateful Christian propaganda against Islam. Many people's first response to anti-*Satanic Verses* anger was to suppose that Muslims could not cope with post-modernist imaginative fiction; the scholarly evidence, how-ever, is that the offending images are far from new and belong to an ancient tradition which Muslims have good reason to fear.

Webster makes an important distinction within blasphemy which the debate has overlooked. While some blasphemy is a form of self-liberation, another sort, historically the more common, is an attack upon the faith of others with the express purpose of abusing or declaring enmity (compare the use of sexual words as forms of endearment and as forms of hate and aggression). While the intentions behind *The Satanic Verses* may point to the former, in borrowing so deeply from the traditional Christian demonising of Muslims, the book falls into the second category and re-opens old wounds.

The churches once supported measures punishing blasphemy against the Christian religion, while encouraging abuse and obscenity against Jews and Muslims. It is a mark of maturity, not weakness, that many Christians, even when easy about blasphemies against their own religion, now recognise the need for a new law against insult and incitement to hatred against minority religions. This conflict of principle is felt even more acutely amongst the non-religious, for 'progressive' opinion is clearly divided between the liber-tarians, many of whom are contemptuous of traditional religion, and cultural pluralists who favour such a law, not on religious grounds but by appealing to equality and social harmony.

It is important to be clear that this is a division within liberalism, not between liberalism and something else. The soul of liberalism is the subject of a contest by the rival claims of libertarianism and pluralism. As the three Comission for Racial Equality books reveal, while libertarianism is dominant in the quality press (Webster's analysis of which should be widely read as a case study of unconscious bias in the higher reaches of journalism), its arguments are far from convincing (CRE, 1990c).

The book is polemical and hard-hitting, but to a constructive purpose. It ends with a plea that recalls George Eliot, for ordinary human sensitivity and the exercise of that imagination by which we lift ourselves out of a moral panic and think ourselves into the lives of other people. As an A-level student I was taught that this moral imagination lay at the heart of 'the great tradition'; it still seems a more worthwhile ideal than the pursuit of a post-modern Utopia where, as Webster observes, everybody is free to abuse and insult everybody else because words cease to wound and insults cease to hurt.

Source: *The Independent*, 19 June 1990.

A Review of **Sacrilege versus Civility**, M M Ahsan and A R Kidwai (eds), The Islamic Foundation

The antagonists over *The Satanic Verses* have a hare and tortoise quality about them. While the libertarian hare went in at top speed, it has been overtaken by the Muslim tortoise. The former dominates the media space, but the output of books and journal articles, which far from trailing off seems to be growing, is predominantly anti-Rushdie and by criticising Orientalism and secularism has widened the basis of opposition. This collection marks a further advance for the tortoise.

Its perspective allows a story to be told that continues to go unreported. How many know, for example, that a petition of 60,000 signatures was presented to the publishers months before the Bradford book-burning, let alone the *fatwa*?

The quantity of Muslim arguments assembled here is impressive and rebuts the view that the affair is a Battle against Ignorance. Yet what is presented is a flawed view, both of civility and of Salman Rushdie's offence. To start with, it is unclear who stands for civility. From the title it would seem to include anybody who opposes the sacrilegious nature of *The Satanic Verses*, but the chapter 'Voices of Civility' consists of pieces by those who stand between the opposed camps of irreverent libertarianism and religious dogmatism, and who categorically condemn the *fatwa*. Underlying this ambiguity is a deeper question which the book does not address. Just as there are illiberal ways of defending liberalism, can there be uncivil ways of defending civility? The avoidance of this question has bedevilled the post-fatwa campaign. The appeal to civility was and is the Muslim moral high ground, but it is no point pretending that Muslims always occupied it.

The editors argue for the jurisprudential validity of the *fatwa*, but argue that as Islamic courts have no jurisdiction in Britain, the sentence of the *fatwa* cannot be carried out on British soil. This is a familiar view but ignores the most basic objection of natural justice, namely that a person cannot be sentenced without a trial: a *fatwa* after all, is only a learned *opinion* and not, as the late Ayatollah Khomeini claimed 'a verdict of execution'. Yet the *fatwa*, as the Friends of Salman Rushdie studiously ignore, was a direct response to

75

the deaths in the riots of Islamabad and Srinigar; to talk of it being 'lifted' without acknowledging the deaths that gave rise to it shows too little political intelligence, not to mention compassion. This could also be said about last week's speech at Columbia, in which Mr Rushdie revived his enthusiasm for a paperback edition.

The confusion the *fatwa* has caused is linked to the uncertainty about the crime the author has committed. The editors describe it as 'a simple issue of blasphemy and profanity' but also as one of creating *fitna*, deep social discord. These are two different crimes with two different punishments. While the Qur'an lays down ostracism and non-retaliation of insult in the first case, someone who creates *fitna* may, in the extreme case of armed attack, warrant capital punishment.

It is perhaps inevitable that books of this sort are crafted to simplify rather than pursue the issues. This one follows the editorial policy, pioneered by *The Rushdie File* and dominant in the media, of excluding Muslim dissent over the *fatwa*, though it at least has the merit of a most helpful bibliography which lists what is edited out.

The area of maximum agreement in the book lies in the judgement that *The Satanic Verses* is a deliberate, mercenary act of Islamophobia. I doubt all three aspects of this judgement. Money was not the motive, nor was blasphemy the intention. The affair was the outcome of a cultural lampoon that went out of control, as the author became intoxicated in the literary possibilities and by his own bravura. *The Satanic Verses* is a product of a cultural sickness, and while Islamphobia is certainly at work, the real sickness is militant irreverence. Rushdie wished to caricature, and was seduced by the norms of contemporary literary culture to go too far.

For all its usefulness as a source book, this collection fails to consider how not just sacrilege but also religious anger can undermine the norms of civility. If there is an argument for legislation against incitement to religious hatred, it is that society has to take seriously what significant sections of it deem hurtful *and* that, once provoked, religious passion can consume civil society.

Source: *The Independent,* 16 December 1991.

A Review of **Islamic Fundamentalism**, Youssef M Choueiri, Pinter

One of the not altogether minor effects of Khomeini's revolution has been the explosion of western interest in Muslim political thought. Western writing on this topic in the past decade may exceed the amount published in the previous 1,400 years. Of course, many of these books are superficial or polemical or both. Titles such as *The Dagger of Islam* and *Ayatollah Khomeini's Mein Kampf* suggest that impartiality and objectivity may not be among the primary features of this corpus. Youssef Choueiri's book is in a new series, 'Themes in Right-Wing Politics and Ideology', which is advertised as 'unbiased, scholarly, up-to-date'. Choueiri lives up to the promise of scholarship and while the book is for the most part intelligent and descriptive, it is equally clear that he is deeply worried by the politics under study.

A puzzling departure from the scholarly consensus, and one that may well reflect a bias, is Choueiri's definition of his subject. For him, Islamic fundamentalism consists of three movements, revivalism, reformism and radicalism, which rather conveniently belong to different periods of history. While the first refers to 18th and 19th century attempts to return to the warrior puritanism of Abd al-Wahhabi, and the last to the anti-imperialist radicalism of Khomeini, Hizbollah and the Muslim Brotherhood, it is Choueiri's contention that the reformism of 19th-century men such as Sayyid Ahmed Khan and Mohammed Abduh is also a form of fundamentalism.

This is odd, because while fundamentalism is about purity of doctrine and a return to an original ahistorical truth, the reformists emphasised the importance of historical change, of modernity and learning from the West. Moreover, their educational, social and political doctrines were right-wing only if J. S. Mill or Matthew Arnold were right-wing. Nor, indeed, do the reformers fall within Choueiri's definition of fundamentalism as a 'rejection of secularism in all its schools and manifestations', for their intention was to make Islam compatible with limited forms of secularism and bring Muslim social elites into contact with modern intellectual and social forces — purposes which they achieved.

They failed, however, to create anything durable that was distinctively Islamic or worthy of western ideals. For, as Choueiri points out, the rhetoric of liberalism created not a democratically progressive polity but, rather, a system of patronage dominated by absentee landlords, the army and the bureaucracy. The problem came to be perceived, however, not only as a failure to catch up with the West, but that the very attempt to do so threatened to destroy the ideal of Islamic polities and so Islam as a political force. It is the recent response to this threat, with in its uncompromising rejection of secular statehood, democracy and individual rights in favour of *Jihad* and *Shari'a,* that most people will have no difficulty in recognising as fundamentalism.

It is to this radicalism that most of the book is devoted and Choueiri has many sound and interesting things to say. (His focus here as elsewhere is on Arab Islam, so that just as Abduh features larger than Sayyid A Khan or Iqbal, so he has more on Qutb than Mawdudi or Khomeini: this obscures the fact that Arabs form only about 15 per cent of the *Ummah,* 40 per cent of which is in the Indian sub-continent.) There is the interplay between Islamic fundamentalism as a totalitarian ideology and the two leading western totalitarian ideologies, Marxism and Fascism. For, besides secular nationalism, one of the immediate targets of Islamic radicals was Marxism, the most popular of the militant western ideologies among Third World intellectuals in the third quarter of this century. Fascism contributed more directly in terms of ideas of party structure as well as a critique of liberal democracy and finance capitalism.

77

Choueiri rightly notes that this radicalism is creative rather than imitative of a supposedly golden age; the best example of which is Khomeini's breathtaking imposition of rule by Ayatollahs, for which there is about as much justification in Islam as for the dictatorship of the proletariat. For these reasons Choueiri is inclined to conclude that these 'back to *Shari'a*' militants are just a modern revolutionary grouping draped in holy robes.

This is, however, to see too much in terms of the West. For all his political acumen, Choueiri fails to give weight to the role of religion. The fact that Islam is able to inspire a political movement — any political movement — is ultimately because that religion (in contrast to those in the west) remains a living reality to its adherents and a source of collective strength and comfort in a time of social crisis. Just as the West is not the source of all the problems of Muslim societies, so, too, it cannot be the source of all the remedies — hence the failure of the two biggest imports, nationalism and Marxism. The current restlessness and resurgence are best understood not as a search for theocracy but as part of the aspiriation of non-western societies to re-establish lines of continuity with epochs before the period of western domination. Choueiri rightly criticises Muslims for a lack of historical consciousness and criticism, yet he himself operates from a left-wing position which uses unhistorical concepts like progress and 'progressive currents'. It is to be hoped that the current collapse of Marxism-Leninism will free scholars from interpreting the world in terms of at least one western myth.

Source: *The Times Higher Education Supplement*, 14 September 1990.

10

Goodbye Alabama:
notes for a new anti-racism

Now that *The Satanic Verses* agitation, the jihad and the counter-jihad have been off the front pages for a number of weeks, it is time to ask why the Muslim campaign, including the largest ethnic minority demonstrations in Britain, remained unreported in the national media for so long? After being so boringly unnewsworthy how come it was perceived to be so shocking as to be vehemently denounced as Nazi? Are there wider currents of thought and feeling amongst ethnic minorities, of which the Muslim anger may be only one example? What does the future hold?

It is now common knowledge that intense Muslim lobbying and large demonstrations had been taking place since October 1988. That they were invisible to the national media until the middle of January 1989 was not the result of an accidental oversight but rooted in how educated opinion understands race issues. Their invisibility, paralleled by many other cases such as the virtual absence of Asian faces in the TUC's beautiful collection of 'black' people in its Anti-Racism resource book or by the exclusion of Asians in Linbert Spencer's recent Radio 4 programme on equality in employment, stems directly from a mode of looking at non-white people. For in the main, Asian and other ethnic minorities are only granted a shadowy existence as statistical 'blacks', as victims of racism but with no identity or consciousness of their own. They cannot but be invisible and unheard if they should become agitated by issues to do with their own being, rather than by what white people think of their 'race'. For in order to see something we need to look for it; in order to look for it we must admit the possibility of its existence. For too many politically informed people in this country Asians are a welcome addition to black statistics but cannot be accepted on their own terms.

The marginalisation of Asian experience, wittingly or otherwise, follows as a natural consequence of the philosophy of race relations which in the 1980s rather successfully marketed the idea of an Alabama-like Britain consisting of two races, whites and blacks, and of the latter as a potentially revolutionary underclass politically attracted to all the radical and libertarian tendencies in white society. Laughable as these ideas will seem, except perhaps to those who have been in hibernation this winter, they have until recently enjoyed an orthodoxy amongst the Left, to challenge which in public is to risk ex-communication or worse. The politics based on these ideas reached its peak in the capture of the GLC and in getting six or seven Labour constituencies with a real chance of returning a Labour MP in 1987 to adopt a 'black' candidate. The ideas still have a lot of political life but are clearly in decline, partly because events keep proving them false and partly because of the Government's attack on local government, the set of institutions where these ideas have been most at work. That one of their latest expressions is Black Section's declaration that, despite their 2.5:1 population ratio, Asian and African-Caribbean MPs should be in a 50:50 proportion, underlies the institutionalised inequality of Asians that this movement represents.

With a climate influenced and in some quarters dominated by this anti-racist perspective it has been difficult for moderate ethnic minority opinion to express itself and to gain media space. While instant publicity was guaranteed, and not just in the tabloid press, to the wilder reaches of Black Sections, more representative opinion has found it consistently difficult to meet the criteria of newsworthiness. Media interest, reflecting the social policy paradigm of the 1980s, has been narrowly circumscribed by racism and anti-racism: ethnic minorities are of interest if and only if they can be portrayed as victims of or threat to white society. This 'radicals and criminals' paradigm, a kind of yellow star that minority persons have to wear on their coat before they have access to the media, is perhaps best epitomised in the deportation of Viraj Mendis. Not only was that the dominant race story in the media in the first half of January, when the unreported anger against *The Satanic Verses* was spreading from mosque to mosque, but Mendis managed to combine in his person both prongs of the fork, 'radical and criminal'.

What was clear but unremarked about Mendis was that though his case was made a cause célèbre by the Workers Revolutionary Party and some radical Christians, he could not win the support of a single Asian community. Asians watched the episode with distaste (how could anyone in Sri Lanka want to kill him when no one there had heard of him and he had not been in the country during the period of the troubles?) knowing full well that hundreds of more deserving causes would get far less or no publicity.

The Muslim agitation against *The Satanic Verses* began almost straight away — obliging the Indian government to ban the book within a few days of its launch — but because it was confined to behind the scenes lobbying it, unlike the book, attracted no media attention. However, even when Muslims began to take to the streets, as in Bolton's 8,000-strong march on December 2, they were determined to be orderly and thereby doomed themselves to continuing invisibility. They found themselves silenced by the racially dis-criminatory judgements that lie at the heart of how race is reported and

80

theorised about. Faced with this powerlessness, the unfortunate but true conclusion the organisers reached was that they would remain unheeded till something shocking and threatening was done.

This led to a book-burning publicity stunt. That started a reaction with the libertarian-left which, when such stunts were interpreted through a prism lent by the Ayatollah, culminated into hysterical denunciations of the demonstrators as Nazis! How demonstrations noteworthy for their peacefulness and lack of attacks on property, police or bystanders could be compared to wholesale ransacking of libraries, and to bully-boy intimidation and beatings, was never explained. 'Nazi' is the strongest term of political abuse in most people's vocabulary and it does not require much intelligence to see what its effects are going to be on a community which is deeply offended and feels itself marooned in a sea of incomprehension. When those who have no qualms about the burning of symbols of living people or democracy, such as effigies of a Prime Minister or a national flag, declare a counter-jihad on those who protest by burning a book, the casualty, in the polarisation which ensues, is moderate Muslim attempts to find constructive ways of channelling anger. Just as on an earlier occasion, when some of the similar forces were at work but the Left played a different role, moderate Muslim opinion found itself undermined in a pincer movement by the mullahs and the Left — though the avowed target was Ray Honeyford.

Some of those who are now concerned about the social dangers of Islamic fundamentalism, and of ethnic minority separatism in general, are doing their best to create what they least want to see. To emigrate to another culture is to initiate a process of change — in oneself, in one's children and in one's children's children. This process is extremely difficult and painful, much more so for communities than individuals. Add to that the experience of racism and you have vulnerable and confused and, at moments, angry communities. Rushdie, in his own fantastical way, has portrayed aspects of this perhaps better than anyone, though his fault — and the root cause of the process which ends with his enraging Muslims — is his preference for the subtleties of his own introspective individuality rather than a collective self-expression. He asked himself 'where am I at?' rather than 'where at the present in the process of our inevitable metamorphosis is the community at?' In the way the community has received his book, the second question too has been answered. Part of this answer surely is that western secular individualism is no less threatening, here and globally, to historical communities than western racism; indeed, in the twentieth century it is far more so, for it is far more confident and unapologetically interfering.

The process of communal metamorphosis is likely to be made much worse the greater the pressure there is to assimilate and to do it fast. Nothing is more likely to distort or freeze that process; and if the call of assimilation is accompanied by racial discrimination and social exclusion then you have the worst of all formulas, one which leads to alienation, conflict and a more politicised separatism — as a generation of African-Caribbeans can testify.

A politics which addresses itself to these problems must support the minority psyche and not become an additional abrasive by creating further anxiety about change.

In the 1950s and 1960s it was blithely assumed that non-white individuals, particularly West Indians, would metamorphosise into quasi-whites. It did not happen. It was then assumed in what was the cardinal error of the later period that West Indian and Asian communities would decompose and be reconstructed into 'blacks'. Despite strenuous efforts and much radical passion it has not happened, and it is now clear that it will not happen. Naturally, there is decomposing and reconstruction going on but a politics which forces this down Asian throats will not be accepted and will indeed infuse a cultural freeze or atavism.

Most people can see how the right-wing 'Become British or go home!' attitude is threatening, coercive and likely to produce the insecure and ill-fitting communities it aims to avoid. Yet the Left is blind to its own brand of assimilationism, which may be characterised as 'Become Black and fight racism!'. When Asian communities evaluate the choices on offer — become quasi-whites or quasi-blacks — the former seems less resistible and more attractive in its rewards. Moreover the most conservative, those who have the most distance to travel, will respond by clutching more tightly their former identities even though deep down they know that such ethnic separatism will (of all options) make them the least liked and will serve them and their children worst. But it is in the nature of proud historical identities, and above all communal faiths, that they are cherished and give comfort regardless of what outsiders think; and that they are held on to most fiercely when they come under attack.

Materialist theories of anti-racism typically under-estimate these feelings and the positive role of ethnic pride. The 'black is beautiful' campaign reached far more American blacks than the civil rights campaign and indeed provided a personal and collective psychological dynamic which fed into the former and which enabled blacks to take advantage of the socio-economic opportunities created by the politics. On a smaller scale the same has happened for British blacks. Asian people too need a similar movement of ethnic pride if race equality politics is to be effective. Even though it is obvious that Asian people mainly get drawn into political campaigns when some aspect of their ethnicity is under threat, the Left's chosen strategy of inviting them into its own politics is under the banner 'black' which, for precisely the reasons that people of African ancestry find exciting, stifles Asian ethnic pride. It would be less foolish to offer the Scots 'Cymru' as a basis for Celtic unity.

In a recent BBC Network East telephone poll on the question 'Should Asians be called black?' nearly two-thirds of the over 3,000 who rang in voted No. Asians no longer passively accept whatever they are described as by politicians, bureaucrats and the media but are actively lobbying to be correct-ly referred to. This movement is paralleled by people of African descent who believe they have outgrown the term 'black' and as an expression of their re-discovery of their ethnicity are choosing to be referred to as hyphenated Africans. With Jesse Jackson in the lead and Britain not that far behind, this too will no doubt baffle and grieve the Left. Muslim demands for state-supported Islamic schools are another instance of where the Left is insensitive to ethnic minority assertiveness. But these developments ought not to cause panic: immigrant communities need lines of continuity and space to create centres of their own excellence in order to prevent themselves being overwhelmed by the ubiquitous pressures of assimilation. People who feel more secure in their own identities and in having some ability to control the pace and nature of change are more likely to adapt with confidence and become genuinely bi-cultural. That the process of change should be in a climate of psychological security is to everybody's advantage for it is insecurity that produces conflict.

On the road to social integration, race equality politics have to go through ethnicity not against it. In the 1980s we learnt that the goals could not be achieved by being 'colour-blind' — witness the change of attitudes over the decade to ethnic monitoring. The lesson of the 1990s will, I believe, be that the goals cannot be achieved by being 'ethnicity-blind'. The recent ferment will not have been wholly negative if we come to acknowledge the falsehood of racial dualism and chart a course to a viable ethnic pluralism.

Goodbye Alabama. There is more in Britain than you can understand.

Source: *The Guardian*, 22 May 1989

11

Faith and Citizenship

It is over a century now since the special position of the Church of England was a major political issue. With the disestablishment of its sister churches in Ireland, Wales and Scotland, and civil society opened up to non-conformists, Roman Catholics and Jews throughout the kingdom, the residual privileges of the Church of England, mainly a special relationship with the Monarch and Parliament, ceased to be seen as a threat by non-Anglicans.

Yet the latest wave of interest in constitutional reform is once again making 'establishment' a political issue. Tony Benn's *Commonwealth of Britain Bill*, and *The Constitution of the United Kingdom*, produced by the prestigious and influential centre-left think-tank, the Institute of Public Policy Research, are two examples of reform which propose a root and branch disestablishment, a measure which received overwhelming support at the Liberal Democrat 1990 Conference. Whilst some Anglicans believe that separation from the state will lead to spiritual vigour, the principal argument offered by reformers is that establishment is not compatible with multi-culturalism. The Church of England may be sufficiently broad to reflect most Christian denominations but now that non-Christians are a significant proportion of British believers, to allow one faith to be formally part of the national polity is to treat non-Christians as not truly part of this country.

This is an important argument. For though non-Christian believers form only about four percent of the population (about half of whom are Muslim), they form not a dispersed population but functioning communities, and given that their levels of religious participation is much higher than amongst Christians (for whom it is less than 15%), active non-Christians form up to a quarter of all active believers. These faiths already represent more active members than the Church of England, and if present trends in demography and membership continue, Islam will overtake the Church of England within two or three decades.

The issue, however, is ultimately not about numbers. It is about the *prominence* of the religious affiliation in one's social identity. This will naturally vary from faith to faith, and so some minorities may be less alienated by 'establishment' than others. It may well, therefore, be the case that if faith is the primary identity of any community, then that minority cannot fully identify with and participate in a polity to the extent that it privileges a rival faith.

Yet as far as I know there is not a single statement by any minority faith organisation in favour of disestablishment. The principal minority community, Muslims, have not been shy about identifying obstacles to their full participation in a plural society: they have dismissed models of multi-cultural state education which do not allow space for religious instruction (to the point that some Muslim leaders are openly talking of withholding their taxes if the state will not offer them a choice which includes Muslim schools); and have rejected the liberal offer of equality with Christians by removing from Christians the legal protection from blasphemy which Muslims want to *share* not abolish. On these issues Muslims have conspicuously not argued that their rights depend upon the dispossession of Christian privileges.

This minority perspective of wanting to share the public space without dispossessing Christians of established rights has been carried to its logical conclusion by Chief Rabbi Sacks. In his 1990 Reith Lectures he argued that the emphasis on diversity needs to be balanced by a strong over-arching public culture; if this is to have any religious dimension, it will be that of the Church of England, consequently all minorities ought to support it as a national institution (Sacks, 1991).

Radical secularists, despite their use of the vocabulary of multi-culturalism are no less committed to an over-arching public culture; they seek to establish a unity in diversity by insisting that religion has no official place in the public sphere. But this is to privilege *a* philosophy of religion and thereby to defeat the claim that secularism is the only neutral way of accommodating all varieties of faiths. Why should those who believe, as Muslims do, that their faith entails communal obligations, a public philosophy and political action feel less like second class citizens in a polity like France in which secularism is woven into the national ideology, than in Britain where a minor national church, that all agree is no more than a residue and a token of a historical past, enjoys certain constitutional privileges?

The minimal nature of the Anglican establishment, its relative openness to other denominations and faiths seeking public space and the fact that its very existence is an on-going acknowledgement of the public character of religion are all reasons why it may seem far less intimidating to the minority faiths than a triumphal secularism. Where secularism is already *the* dominant ideology and the national church is marginal, it is dishonest to suggest that religious equality and empowerment of the new minority faiths begins with a critique of establishment. The cause of equality would be much better served by giving all ethno-religious minorities, not as at the moment just Sikhs and Jews, protection against direct discrimination and hateful literature, and by extending the range of religious schools and education within the state system. But this is to concede that religion, no less than gender, race or class, has a place in a secular public culture; that the state must be shaped around the existence of religious, as of other, communities.

As we enter an uncertain and potentially turbulent multi-culturalism, we must seek to use existing, or create new, institutional resources that bring different faiths together. Otherwise we will inevitably create a mentality of: religion divides, the secular unites; or worse still: religion is 'backward' and negative, secularism is progressive; religious people are the problem, secular rule is the solution. Of course, there must be secular unities at individual and group levels. Yet our society will be more divided than it need be and Muslims more demonised than they need be if we do not have in place at least a few (symbolic) centrifugal institutions in which Muslims can participate *qua* Muslims, so that 'Muslim' does not simply become (perceived as) a 'divisive' identity. Muslims are going to press for and get some centripetal institutions. I think it is to everyone's benefit for Muslims also to participate in some centrifugal processes. My fear is that 'progressive' secular reform may, in its ignorance, diminish the opportunities for this coming-together and then blame the subsequent separatism on Muslim backwardness rather than on the exclusionism implicit in radical secularism. Pluralism may turn out to be less 'progressive' than many desire or fear; what is certain is that it is incompatible with radical secularism.

Source: *New Statesman and Society*, July 1992. For a fuller discussion, see Modood 1992c.

Bibliography

Aldrich, H., Jones, T.P. and McEvoy, D. (1984) 'Ethnic advantage and minority business development' in Ward, R and Jenkins, R. (eds) *Ethnic communities in business: strategies for economic survival*, Cambridge: Cambridge University Press: 189-210.

Amin, K. and Richardson, R. (1992) *Politics For All: Equality, Culture and The General Election 1992*, London: The Runnymede Trust.

Ballard, R. (1989) 'Differentiation and disjunction amongst the Sikhs in Britain in Barrier, G. and Dusenberry, V. (eds) *The Sikh Diaspora: migration and the experience beyond Punjab* Columbia, Missouri: South Asia Books: 200-232.

Ballard, R. (1990) 'Migration and kinship: the differential effect of marriage rules on the process of Punjabi migration to Britain, in Clarke, C., Peach, C. and Vertovec, S. (eds) *South Asians Overseas*, Cambridge: Cambridge University Press.

Ballard, R. and Vellins, S. (1985) 'South Asian entrants to British universities: a comparative note', *New Community*, 12(2): 260-265.

Banton, M. (1979) 'It's our country' in Miles, R. and Phizacklea, A. (eds) *Racism and political action in Britain* London: Routhledge & Kegan Paul: 223-246.

Banton, M (1988) *Which Relations are Racial Relations?*, Presidential Address, Royal Anthropological Institute, London.

Banton, M (1989) *Science, Law and Politics in the Study of Racial Relations*, Presidential Address, Anthropological Institute, London.

BBC Radio 4 (1988) Woman's hour, 17 November.

BBC TV (1988) Heart of the Matter, 10 July.

Brennan, J. and McGeevor, P. (1990) *Ethnic minorities and the graduate labour market*, A report by the Council for National Academic Awards for the Commission for Racial Equality, London.

Brown, C. and Gay, P. (1985) *Racial discrimination: 17 years after the Act*, London: Policy Studies Institute.

Cater, J. and Jones, T. (1991) 'Community, Ethnicity and Class Among South Asians in Britain' in Vertovec, S. (ed) *Aspects of South Asian Diaspora*, Oxford University Papers on India, vol. 2, Part 2, New Delhi: Oxford University Press, pp.169-197.

Commission for Racial Equality (1987) *Chartered accountancy training contracts: report of a formal investigation into ethnic minority recruitment*, London.

Commission for Racial Equality (1988a) *Medical school admissions: report of a formal investigation into St. George's Hospital Medical School*, London.

89

Commission for Racial Equality (1988b) 'Ethnic classification system recommended by CRE', Press Statement, 7 December.

Commission for Racial Equality (1990a) 'Formal investigation into chartered accountancy training contract: progress report and information note', London.

Commission for Racial Equality (1990b) *Sorry it's gone: testing for racial discrimination in the private rented housing sector,* London.

Commission for Racial Equality (1990c) Three Discussion Papers: (1) *Law, Blasphemy and the Multi-Faith Society*; (2) *Free Speech*; (3) *Britain: A Plural Society*, London.

Cross, M. (1989) 'African-Caribbeans and Asians are affected differently by British racism', *New Statesman and Society*, 7 April 1989: 35.

Dahya, B (1974), 'The Nature of Pakistani Ethnicity in Industrial Cities in Britain', in A Cohen (ed), *Urban Ethnicity*, London: Tavistock: 77-117.

Dennis, F (1989), 'Called by Africa', *The Listener*, 13 April: 12.

Department of Health (1989a) 'Community medicine and community health service medical staff — England and Wales', London

Department of Health (1989b) 'Statistical bulletin', London

Dolton, P. J., Makepeace, G.H. and Inchley, G.D. (1990) *The early careers of 1980 graduates: earnings, earnings differentials and post-graduate study*, Research Paper No. 78, Department of Employment, London

Duffy, K B and Lincoln, I C, (1990), *Earnings and Ethnicity*, Leicester: Leicester City Council.

East Birmingham Task Force (1989), *East Birmingham Task Force Skills Survey.*

Employment Institute, (1990), 'Racial Equality in the British Labour Market', London.

Field, S. (1987) 'The changing nature of racial disadvantage', *New Community* 14 (1/2): 118-122.

Fielding, N. (1992) 'Cornerstone of Success', *The Independent on Sunday*, Business Section, 12 January, pp.12-13.

Foyster, R. et al (1990 'I landed twice as many jobs as my two friends — but then they are black' *Today*, 11 September.

Fuchs, l.H. (1990) *The American Kaleidoscope: Race, Ethnicity and the Civic Culture*, USA and London: University Press of New England.

Gilroy, P (1989), 'Know What I Mean, Harry?', *New Statesman and Society,* 7 April: 24-25.

Haskey, J. (1990) 'The ethnic minority populations of Great Britain: estimates by ethnic group and country of birth', *Population Trends*, 60 (Summer): 35-38.

Jowell, R. *et al* (1986) *British Social Attitudes: the 1986 Report,* Social and Community Planning Research, London: Gower.

Kogbara, D. (1988) 'When is a black not a black?', *The Independent*, 30 November.

Kramer, J. (1991) 'Letter from Europe', *New Yorker,* 14 January, pp.60-75.

Lal, B B (1983), 'Perspectives on Ethnicity: Old Wine in New Bottles', *Ethnic and Racial Studies* 6(2): 154-173

Lal, B B (1990) *The Romance of Culture in an Urban Civilization: Robert E Park on Race and Ethnic Relations in Cities*, London: Routledge and Kegan Paul.

Maja-Pearce, A. (1990) *How many miles to Babylon?*, London: Heinemann.

Mason, D. (1990) 'A Rose By Any Other Name...? Categorisation, Identity and Social Science', *New Community* 17(1):123-133.

McEvoy, D., Jones, T.P., Cater, J.C. and Aldrich, H.E. (1982) 'Asian immigrant businesses in British cities', British Association for the Advancement of Science, Annual Meeting, September.

McManus, I.C., Richards, P. and Maitlis, S.L. (1989) 'Prospective study of the disadvantage of people from ethnic minority groups applying to medical schools in the United Kingdom', *British Medical Journal* (298): 723-6.

Menski, W. (1983) 'Asian retail trade in England', 8 European conference on modern South Asian studies, Taelbergh, Sweden, July.

Merchant, K. (1991) 'Keeping it in the Family', *Financial Times*, 24 September.

Miles, R (1982), *Racism and Migrant Labour*, London: Routledge and Kegan Paul.

Modood, T. (1988a) 'Who is defining whom?' *New Society*, 4 March.

Modood, T. (1988b) 'Black', racial equality and Asian identity' *New Community* 14(3): 397-404.

Modood, T. (1989) 'Religious anger and minority rights' *Political Quarterly* 60(3): 280-284.

Modood, T (1990a) 'Colour, Class and Culture: the 3 Cs of Race', *Equal Opportunities Review*, 30: 31-33.

Modood, T (1990b) 'British Asian Muslims and the Salman Rushdie Affair', *Political Quarterly* 61(2): 143-160; also in Donald, J. and Rattansi, A. (1992) *'Race', Culture and Difference*, London: Sage.

Modood, T. (1990c) 'Muslims, Incitement to Hatred and the Law', Morrell Conference on Toleration, Pluralism and Multiculturalism at University of York, 17-19 September; the conference papers are to be published as Horton, J. (ed) *Liberalism, Multiculturalism and Toleration*, Macmillan.

Modood, T. (1992a) 'On Not Being White in Britain: Discrimination, Diversity and Commonality' in Taylor, M.J. and Leicester, M. (eds) *Ethics, Ethnicity and Education*, London: Kegan Page.

Modood, T. (1992b) 'Cultural diversity and racial discrimination in employment selection' in Bob Hepple and Erika Szyszczak (eds) *Discrimination: the limits of law?*, London: Mansell.

Modood, T. (1992c) 'Ethno-Religious Minorities, Secularism and the British State', conference on Religion in the Common European Home, 8-11 April, London, to be published in Murphy, T. (ed) *Religious Freedom in Plural Societies* (forthcoming).

Modood, T. (1992d) 'The End of a Hegemony: The Concept of 'Black' and British Asians', Centre for Research in Ethnic Relations Annual Conference 'The Mobilisation of Ethnic Minorities and Ethnic Social Movements in Europe', University of Warwick, 3-5 April.

Modood, T. (forthcoming) 'The Number of Ethnic Minority Students in British Higher Education', *Oxford Review of Education*.

Murphy, D. (1987) *Tales from two cities*, London: John Murray.

Nanton, P. (1989) 'The new orthodoxy: racial categories and equal opportunity policy', *New Community* 15(4): 549-564

Parekh, B. (1990) 'The BASAS residential course', BASAS Bulletin: the newsletter of the British Association for South Asian Studies, 12:1-3.

Park, R E and Miller H A (1921), *Old World Traits Transplanted*, New York: Harper.

Patel, S. (1985) 'Liverpool research biased', *Independent Grocer,* 16 August: 30.

Penman, A. (1990) 'Who needs a bank when the Patels run corner shops plc,' *Today*, 8 October.

Poulter, S (1986) *English Law and Ethnic Minority Customs*, London: Butterworths.

Poulter, S (1989) 'The Significance of Ethnic Minority Customs and Traditions in English Criminal Law', *New Community* 16(1): 121-128.

Poulter, S (1990) 'Cultural Pluralism and its Limits: A Legal Perspective', *Britain: A Plural Society,* London: Commission for Racial Equality: 3-28.

Rafiq, M. (1992) 'Ethnicity and Enterprise: A Comparison of Muslim and Non-Muslim Owned Asian Businesses in the UK', conference on Muslims in Europe, Berliner Institut für Vergleicdende Sozialforschung, Berlin.

Rex, J (1981) 'A Working Paradigm for Race Research', *Ethnic and Racial Studies* 4(1): 10-25.

Rex, J (1986) *Race and Ethnicity*, Milton Keynes: Open University Press.

Rex, J (1988) 'The Urban Sociology of Religion and Islam in Birmingham' in T Gerholm and Y G Lithman (eds), *The New Islamic Presence in Western Europe*, London: Mansell: 206-218.

Rex, J (1989) Review of A Shaw: A Pakistani Community in Britain, *New Community*, 15(2): 305-6.

Rex, J and Moore, R (1967) *Race, Community and Conflict*, London: Oxford University Press for the Institute of Race Relations.

Robinson, V. (1986) *Transients, settlers and refugees: Asians in Britain*, Oxford: Oxford University Press.

Robinson, V. (1988) 'The new Indian middle class in Britain' *Ethnic and Racial Studies*, 11(4): 456-473.

Robinson, V. (1990) 'Roots to mobility: the social mobility of Britain's black population, 1971-87' *Ethnic and Racial Studies*, 13(2): 274-286.

Robinson, V. and Flintoff, I. (1982) 'Asian retailing in Coventry', *New Community*, 10(2): 251-258.

Roy, A. (1988) 'Asians protest, we are not black', *The Sunday Times*, 26 June.

Roy, A. (1990) 'The quiet millionaires' *Telegraph Weekend Magazine*, 25 August: 13-21.

Sacks, J. (1991) *The Persistence of Faith: Religion, Morality and Society in a Secular Age*, The Reith Lectures 1990, London: Weidenfeld and Nicolson.

Skeel, S. (1990) 'Asian majors,' *Management Today*, September: 57-62

Smith, D. (1976) *The facts of racial disadvantage: a national survey,* London: Policy Studies Institute.

Smith, P. (1989) *Race relations survey on behalf of the Bar Council,* London: Social and Community Planning Research.

Smith, S J (1989) *The Politics of 'Race' and Residence,* Cambridge: The Polity Press.

Stone, J (1985) *Racial Conflict in Contemporary Society,* London: Fontana.

Tanna, K. (1990) 'Excellence, equality and educational reform: the myth of South Asian achievement levels' *New Community* (16) 3:349-368.

Today (1990) 24 January: 12.

Uppal, I.S. (1988) 'Black': the word making Asians angry', *Daily Mail,* 28 June.

Vellins, S. (1982) 'South Asian students in British universities: a statistical note ' *New Community* 10(2): 206-212.

Wahhab, I. (1990) 'Asians spurn help of the race relations industry' *Independent on Sunday,* 8 July: 4.

Yekawi, D (1986) *British Racsim, Miseducation and the Afrikan Child,* London: Karnak House.